Supporting Students in a Time of Core Standards

NCTE Editorial Board

Supporting Students in a Time of Core Standards

English Language Arts, Grades 9–12

Sarah Brown Wessling
Johnston High School, Johnston, Iowa

with
Danielle Lillge
The University of Michigan

Crystal VanKooten
The University of Michigan

NCTE
National Council of Teachers of English
1111 W. Kenyon Road, Urbana, Illinois 61801-1096

Manuscript Editor: THERESA KAY
Staff Editor: BONNY GRAHAM
Interior Design: JENNY JENSEN GREENLEAF
Cover Design: PAT MAYER
Cover Background: ISTOCKPHOTO.COM/ARTIOM MUHACIOV

NCTE Stock Number: 49447

Library of Congress Cataloging-in-Publication Data

Wessling, Sarah Brown, 1975–
   Supporting students in a time of core standards : English language arts, grades 9–12 / Sarah Brown Wessling.
        p. cm.
   Includes bibliographical references.
   ISBN 978-0-8141-4944-7 ((pbk))
   1. Language arts (Secondary)--United States. 2. Education--Standards--United States. I. Title
   LB1631.W358 2011
   428.4'071--dc23

2011029956

Contents

Acknowledgments

I am grateful to Kent Williamson and the National Council of Teachers of English for supporting this work and for reminding us all that we have compasses of best practice to hold on to in times of change. For impeccable vision and a model of advocacy at its finest, Anne Ruggles Gere guided this entire series with precision and affirmation of the ways in which we must continue to grow in thinking and learning. Always with just the right question to provoke our thinking and an incredible eye for the details that led us all to cohesion, Crystal VanKooten has been a gift. Likewise Danielle Lillge, whose wisdom and tenacity continue to reveal themselves through the layers of our thinking as she gently unpacks and gives life to the classrooms and teachers who heroically emerge in this book. But most important, we are all indebted to the teachers who so graciously opened up their classroom doors to share their practices and remind us all what it means to teach with integrity and students in mind. Finally, to my greatest teachers: my husband, children, and family, who continue to remind me why we do this work.

Observing the CCSS

I

⊚ Introduction

Not long ago I was driving a van filled with middle school soccer players and heard a voice from the back say, "I hate, I hate, I hate the MEAP." (The MEAP is Michigan's state test of math and English language arts [ELA].) I recognized the voice as that of a friend of my daughter, a good student, diligent in every way. Her class had just spent a month preparing for and then taking the MEAP, and she was feeling frustrated by the time spent and anxious about her performance.

That plaintive voice reminded me of concerns I've heard expressed about the latest chapter in the standards movement. The appearance of the Common Core State Standards (CCSS) has aroused a variety of responses, some of them filled with anxiety and resentment. It's easy to get worried about issues of alignment, curricular shifts, and new forms of assessment. And it's frustrating, after carefully developing state ELA standards, to have to put them aside in favor of the CCSS. As one teacher put it, "The CCSS are less detailed than the standards they are replacing." Another lamented, "How are teachers supposed to have time to rewrite curriculum and realign lessons to CCSS now that the state has taken away our meeting times?"

Yet, responses to the CCSS have also been positive. Some teachers have said that the grade-specific standards are helpful because they provide useful details about learning goals for students. Others have noted that the CCSS can help them address the needs of transient students because teachers in different schools will be addressing similar learning goals. Still others have commented that the CCSS can provide a lens through which they can examine their own teaching practices. As one teacher put it, "Looking at the standards made me realize that I wasn't giving much attention to oral language." Another said, "I think they provide more opportunities for higher-order thinking and an authentic application of the content we teach."

Regardless of teacher responses, the CCSS are now part of the educational landscape. But these standards do not replace the principles that guide good teaching. Some things remain constant regardless of new mandates. One such principle is that teachers think first of their students, trying to understand their learning needs, developing effective ways to meet those needs, and continually affirming that the needs are being met. This book, like all four volumes in this series, is written with and by teachers who remain deeply committed to their students and their literacy learning. It is a book addressed to teachers like you. You may be an experienced teacher who has established ways of fostering literacy learning, or you may be a relative newcomer to the classroom who is looking for ideas and strategies, but that you are holding this book in your hands says that you put students at the center of your teaching.

No one knows as much about your students as you do. You understand the community that surrounds the school and helps to shape their life experiences. You have some information about their families and may even know their parents or guardians personally. You can tell when they are having difficulty and when they are feeling successful. You have watched their body language, scanned their faces, listened to their voices, and read enough of their writing to have some ideas about what matters to them. Your knowledge about your students guides the instructional choices you make, and it shapes your response to any mandate, including the CCSS.

Your knowledge about students is probably connected to your knowledge of assessment. You know the importance of finding out what students have learned and what they still need to learn. You probably already know about the importance of authentic assessment, measures of learning that are connected with work students can be expected to do outside of class as well as in it. No doubt you use formative assessment, measures of learning that give students feedback rather than grades and help you know what they still need to learn. For example, you probably make sure that students respond to one another's written drafts as they develop a finished piece of writing. You may have individual conferences with student writers or offer marginal comments and suggestions on their drafts. Or perhaps you meet individually with students to hear them read aloud or tell you about what they have been reading. Whatever type of formative assessment you use, you probably use it to guide the decisions you make about teaching.

You may have read or heard about the Principles for Learning adopted by NCTE and other subject-matter associations, principles that position literacy at the heart of learning in all subjects, describe learning as social, affirm the value of learning about learning, urge the importance of assessing progress, emphasize new media, and see learning in a global context. These principles, like others articulated by NCTE, provide a North Star to guide instruction regardless of specific mandates, and you probably recognize that teaching based on such principles will foster student achievement, including achievement of the CCSS.

Because you are concerned about the learning of *all* of your students, you probably try to find ways to affirm the wide variety of racial, ethnic, socioeconomic, and religious backgrounds that students bring into the classroom. No doubt you are interested in taking multiple approaches to reading, writing, speaking, and listening so that you can engage as many students as possible. Taking this stance convinces you that continual growth and innovation are essential to student achievement, especially when new standards are being introduced.

This book is designed to support you in meeting the challenges posed by the CCSS. It stands on the principle that standards do not mean standardization or a one-size-fits-all approach to teaching. It assumes that inspirational teaching—teaching that engages students as critical problem solvers who embrace multiple ways of representing knowledge—can address standards most effectively. It celebrates new visions of innovation and the renewal of long-held visions that may have become buried in the midst of day-to-day obligations. It reinforces a focus on student learning by demonstrating ways of addressing these standards while also adhering to NCTE principles of effective teaching. It does this by, first, examining the CCSS to identify key features and address some of the most common questions they raise. The second section of this book moves into the classrooms of individual teachers, offering snapshots of instruction and showing how teachers developed their practices across time. These classroom snapshots demonstrate ways to address learning goals included in the CCSS while simultaneously adhering to principles of good teaching articulated by NCTE. In addition to narratives of teaching, this section includes charts that show, quickly, how principles and standards can be aligned. Finally, this section offers suggestions for professional development, both for individuals and for teachers who participate in communities of practice. Thanks to NCTE's online resources, you can join in a community of practice that extends across local and state boundaries, enabling you to share ideas and strategies with colleagues from many parts of the country. Embedded throughout this section are student work samples and many other artifacts, and NCTE's online resources include many more materials, from which you can draw and to which you can contribute. The final section of this book recognizes that effective change requires long-term planning as well as collaboration among colleagues, and it offers strategies and materials for planning units of study articulating grade-level expectations and mapping yearlong instruction.

Voices in the back of your mind, like the "I hate, I hate" voice in the back of my van, may continue to express frustrations and anxieties about the CCSS, but I am confident that the teachers you will meet in this book along with the ideas and strategies offered will reinforce your view of yourself as a professional educator charged with making decisions about strategies and curriculum to advance the learning of your students.

Anne Ruggles Gere
Series Editor

1

Demystifying the Common Core State Standards

I always approach the standards with my students in mind. I try to come up with a lesson that I think will be interesting for students. Then I'll sit down and say, which standards am I covering, which should I be covering that I'm not covering? I see part of my job as trying to get the kids that aren't interested to be interested. The whole point is to help the kids, that's the whole reason I do it. You have to continue to try new things, to be comfortable with what you're doing, and to try to reach as many kids as possible. That's the sole purpose of what I do. I'll do it any way I can.

—STEVE BODNAR, *High School English Teacher*

Putting students at the center means thinking first about the kinds of learning experiences we want them to have, and since forty-plus states have adopted the Common Core State Standards (CCSS) (see http://www .corestandards.org/the-standards), many teachers will need to think about student learning in light of these standards. First, though, it will be helpful to understand where these standards came from and what they actually say.

The CCSS are part of a long-term movement toward greater accountability in education that stretches back to the early 1990s. In this line of thinking, accountability focuses on student achievement rather than, say, time spent in classrooms or materials used, and standards like the ones developed by states beginning in the 1990s have been used to indicate what students should achieve. Because of this emphasis, standards are often equated with educational transformation, as in "standards-based school reform." Proponents of standards-based reform have differing views of how standards should be used. Some assume that standards can lead to investments and curricular changes that will improve schools, while others see them as linked to testing that has little to do with allocating resources that will change schools for the better. This book operates from the assumption that ELA teachers can use standards as a lens through which they can examine and improve the *what* and *how* of instruction, and the vignettes in Section II demonstrate how teachers are doing this.

The CCSS for English Language Arts and Mathematics, then, are the latest in a series of standards-based school reform initiatives. They were coordinated by the National Governors Association Center for Best Practices (NGA Center) and the Council of Chief State School Officers (CCSSO) to prepare US students for both college and the workplace. This partnership of state governors and state school superintendents worked with Achieve Inc., an education reform organization founded in 1996 and based in Washington, DC, to develop CCSS. Funding for their work was provided by the Bill and Melinda Gates Foundation, the Charles Steward Mott Foundation, and other private groups. Each state decided whether to adopt the CCSS, and the US Department of Education created an incentive by linking adoption of the CCSS to Race to the Top (RTT), requiring states that applied for RTT funds to adopt the CCSS. When the CCSS were released in June of 2010, more than forty states had already agreed to adopt them.

Web 1.1

Throughout this volume, you will find links, reproducibles, interactive opportunities, and other online resources indicated by this icon. Go online to www.ncte.org/books /supp-students-9-12 to take advantage of these materials.

Web 1.2

For updates on the development of CCSS assessments, check online.

In the states that have formally adopted them, the CCSS will replace state standards. States may add 15 percent, which means that some elements of state standards could be preserved or new standards could be developed. The full text of the ELA standards, along with other explanatory materials, is available online at http://www.corestandards .org/the-standards/english-language-arts-standards.

In September of 2010, two consortia of states, the Partnership for the Assessment of Readiness for College and Careers (PARCC) and the SMARTER Balanced Assessment Consortium, were funded—also with RTT monies—to develop assessments to accompany the CCSS, and these assessments are scheduled for implementation in 2014. At this point it is impossible to know precisely what the assessments will include, but preliminary documents indicate that formative assessment may play a role, that computers may be involved in both administration and scoring, and that some parts of the assessment, such as writing, may occur over multiple days.

I don't have time to read through the entire CCSS document, so can you give me a quick summary?

The ELA standards for grades 9–12 address four basic strands for ELA: reading, writing, speaking and listening, and language. Although each is presented separately, the introduction to the CCSS in English Language Arts advocates for an integrated model of literacy in which all four dimensions are interwoven. In addition, the CCSS for grades 9–12 include standards for history/social studies and science and technical subjects, which have reading and writing strands. Each strand has overarching Anchor Standards, which are translated into grade-specific standards. Figure 1.1 shows the structural relationship of the two.

The content of the two is similarly linked. For example, the 6–12 Anchor Standards for writing include the category "text types and purposes," and one of the Anchor Standards in this category reads, "write arguments to support claims in an analysis of substantive topics or texts, using valid reasoning and relevant and sufficient evidence." One of the three 9–10 grade-specific standards that address this Anchor Standard includes the following:

- Introduce precise claim(s), distinguish the claim(s) from alternate or opposing claims, and create an organization that establishes clear relationships among claim(s), counterclaims, reasons, and evidence
- Develop claim(s) and counterclaims fairly, supplying evidence for each while pointing out the strengths and limitations of both in a manner that anticipates the audience's knowledge level and concerns

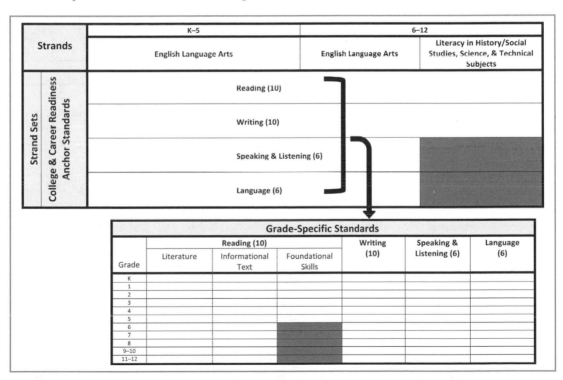

FIGURE 1.1: Structural relationships of the CCSS.

- Use words, phrases, and clauses to link the major sections of the text, create cohesion, and clarify the relationships between claim(s) and reasons
- Establish and maintain a formal style and objective tone while attending to the norms and conventions of the discipline in which they are writing
- Provide a concluding statement or section that follows from and supports the argument presented

To see examples of how teachers implement these and other grade-specific standards in their classrooms, turn to Section II of this book.

Web 1.3

Needless to say, the introduction of the CCSS raises many questions for teachers and other instructional leaders. New mandates such as the CCSS can generate misconceptions and even myths, so it is important to look at the standards themselves. Because the implementation of the CCSS is an ongoing process, and because assessment is still under development, the online community associated with this book provides updates as well as a place to share ideas and experiences.

What is the relationship between the CCSS and the ones my state already developed?

There may well be some overlap between the CCSS and the standards developed by your state, particularly when you look at the more global goals of the Anchor Standards. Because it is possible to supplement the CCSS with up to 15 percent of state standards, some state standards may be preserved, but generally in states that have formally adopted the CCSS these new standards will replace existing state ones. The timing of implementing CCSS varies from one state to another, with some states shifting immediately and others doing it over a year or two.

There are some distinct differences between the CCSS and state standards:

- First, they are intended to be used by all states so that students across the United States will be expected to achieve similar goals, even though they may reach them by different routes.
- The interdisciplinary emphasis of including literacy standards for history, science, social studies, and technical subjects in grades 6–12 makes the CCSS different from most state ELA standards.
- The CCSS emphasize *rigor* and connect it with what is called *textual complexity*, a term that refers to levels of meaning, quantitative readability measures, and reader variables such as motivation and experience.

- The CCSS position students as increasingly independent learners, frequently describing tasks they should perform "without assistance."

Will the CCSS create a national curriculum?

No. CCSS focuses on results, on what students should know and be able to do rather than the specific means for achieving learning goals. As the introduction to the CCSS states on page 4, "the Standards leave room for teachers, curriculum developers and states to determine how these goals should be reached and what additional topics should be addressed. . . . Teachers are thus free to provide students with whatever tools and knowledge their professional judgment and experience identify as most helpful for meeting the goals set out in the Standards." In other words, the CCSS focus on what students should take away from schooling, but they stipulate that teachers should decide what to teach, how to teach it, and when and for how long to teach it. The CCSS acknowledge that teachers know what students bring to the classroom and how they learn best. Ongoing professional development, especially communities of learning with colleagues, will ensure that teachers have the content knowledge and expertise with instructional strategies to foster effective student learning.

I've heard that the CCSS includes lists of *exemplar* texts. Isn't that going to create a national curriculum?

The CCSS do include lists of texts on page 58 that illustrate what is called text complexity for each grade-level band. At the 9–10 level, for instance, the texts include both literary and informational texts. Among the literary selections are *The Tragedy of Macbeth* by William Shakespeare, "Ozymandias" by Percy Bysshe Shelley, "The Raven" by Edgar Allan Poe, "The Gift of the Magi" by O. Henry, *The Grapes of Wrath* by John Steinbeck, *Fahrenheit 451* by Ray Bradbury, and *The Killer Angels* by Michael Shaara. Informational texts include "Speech to the Second Virginia Convention" by Patrick Henry, "Farewell Address" by George Washington, "State of the Union Address" by Franklin Delano Roosevelt, "Letter from Birmingham Jail" by Martin Luther King Jr., and "Hope, Despair and Memory" by Elie Wiesel.

 Web 1.4

However, these texts are simply offered as examples of topics and genres that teachers might include, not as specific texts to be adopted in all classrooms. Teachers need to select texts appropriate for their own students and for the context in which they work. As the vignettes in Section II show, teachers can use a variety of texts to address the CCSS—Maya Angelou's *I Know Why the Caged Bird Sings* and Peter Kuper's *The Metamorphosis* are just two of them. The vignettes also show that these central or fulcrum texts work best when surrounded by contextual and texture texts that add perspective and meaning. For example, *The Great Gatsby* takes on new dimensions when read next to Nella Larsen's *Passing* and texts about the Eighteenth Amendment, which legalized Prohibition.

What more do we know about text complexity?

In Appendix A, page 4, the CCSS define text complexity as "level of meaning, structure, language conventionality and clarity, knowledge demands, word frequency, sentence length [all in the context of] student knowledge, motivation and interest." This definition is expanded in a three-part model—qualitative dimensions, quantitative dimensions, and reader and task considerations. The quantitative dimension refers to features, such as word length or frequency, sentence length, and cohesion, that can be calculated by computers. The qualitative dimension refers to levels of meaning, structure, language conventions, and knowledge demands that cannot be measured well by machines but require careful attention from experienced readers/teachers. The reader and task considerations in Appendix A, page 4 include student motivation, knowledge, and experience as well as the purpose for reading, again, features that can be discerned by teachers "employing their professional judgment, experience and knowledge of their students and the subject."

It is worth noting that the CCSS acknowledge the limitations of this model of text complexity, particularly for literary forms such as poetry. Quantitative measures, for example, simply don't provide useful information about the relative complexity of a poem. Nor do they provide a useful measure of the complexity of much narrative fiction. As the CCSS observe in Appendix A, page 8, "some widely used quantitative measures, including the Flesch-Kincaid Grade Level test and the Lexile Framework for Reading, rate the Pulitzer Prize–winning novel *Grapes of Wrath* as appropriate for grades 2–3." This means that teachers need to play a key role in deciding what constitutes textual complexity for their students.

What does *rigor* mean in this context?

Rigor is used in relation to text complexity. For example, in describing the reading standards for literature on pages 11 and 36, the CCSS include this sentence: "Rigor is also infused through the requirement that students read increasingly complex texts through the grades." Rigor refers to the goal of helping students to continue developing their capacities as readers so that with each passing year they build upon skills and understandings developed during the previous year.

Teachers who immerse their students in rich textual environments, require increasing amounts of reading, and help students choose ever more challenging texts will address rigor as it is defined by the CCSS. This means keeping students at the center, motivating them to continually develop as writers and readers, and engaging them in literacy projects that are relevant to their lives. When students feel personal connections, they are much more willing to wrestle with complex topics/texts/questions. Student engagement, then, offers the best route to rigor.

Will implementing the CCSS mean eliminating literature in favor of "informational texts"?

It is true that the CCSS give significant attention to nonfiction, and on page 5, the introduction includes this statement: "Fulfilling the standards . . . requires much greater attention to a specific category of informational text—literary nonfiction." According to the CCSS, the amount of nonfiction should be increased as students mature so that by the time they are seniors in high school, 70 percent of their reading should be nonfiction. But it is also true that CCSS describe literacy development as a responsibility to be shared by teachers across multiple disciplines, so this doesn't mean that 70 percent of reading in ELA classes should be nonfiction. The standards for history/social studies, science, and technological subjects demonstrate how responsibility for reading nonfiction should be spread across multiple courses.

To reinforce this point, on page 5, the CCSS introduction underscores the importance of teaching literature: "Because the ELA classroom must focus on literature (stories, drama, and poetry) as well as literary nonfiction, a great deal of informational reading . . . must take place in other classes." The CCSS advocate the combination of adding more nonfiction to the curriculum in history/social studies, science, and technical subjects along with including more nonfiction in ELA classes. This combination still leaves plenty of space for literature in ELA classes.

Do the CCSS advocate separating reading, writing, speaking, listening, and language from one another?

No. Although the standards are listed separately, the CCSS propose an integrated model of literacy. On page 4, the introduction explains, "Although the Standards are divided into Reading, Writing, Speaking, and Listening, and Language strands for conceptual clarity, the processes of communication are closely connected as reflected throughout this document. For example, Writing Standard 9 requires that students be able to write about what they read." This integrated approach fits well with NCTE principles and with the ELA standards developed by many states.

Formative evaluation is becoming increasingly important in my school. How do the CCSS address this?

Since the assessment portion of the CCSS is currently under development, it is impossible to know how it will address formative evaluation. The preliminary descriptions offered by the PARCC consortium use the phrase "through course components," which is described as "actionable data that teachers can use to plan and adjust instruction." This suggests that formative evaluation could well be part of the CCSS assessment.

This could be good news because formative evaluation is assessment *for* learning, not assessment *of* learning. When assessment helps teachers understand where students are having difficulty, as well as where they understand clearly, it is possible to adjust instruction to address the areas of difficulty. Research shows that formative assessment can be a powerful means of improving achievement, particularly for students who typically don't do well in school.

Web 1.5

Because assessments for the CCSS will be under development until 2014, it is worthwhile to monitor and perhaps contribute to their evolving shape. The websites for PARCC and SMARTER Balanced each include a list of the "governing states," and once you have determined which consortium your state is participating in, you can get in touch with the state representative(s) to learn more.

What do the CCSS say about English language learners and/or students with special needs?

In a section titled "What Is Not Covered by the Standards" on page 6, the CCSS explain, "It is also beyond the scope of the Standards to define the full range of supports appropriate for English language learners and for students with special needs. At the same time, all students must have the opportunity to learn and meet the same high standards if they are to access the knowledge and skills necessary in their post-high school lives." This section goes on to say, "Each grade will include students who are still acquiring English. For those students, it is possible to meet the standards in reading, writing, speaking and listening without displaying native-like control of conventions and vocabulary." Based on this, we might assume some flexibility in applying the CCSS to English language learners.

The statement on page 6 about students with special needs takes a similar position: "The Standards should also be read as allowing for the widest possible range of students to participate fully from the outset and as permitting appropriate accommodations to ensure maximum participation of students with special education needs." Clearly the CCSS provide only limited guidance for implementing the standards with English language learners and students with special needs.

Am I wrong to think that the CCSS will undercut teacher authority?

Probably. The CCSS make frequent reference to teachers' professional judgment and emphasize that teachers and other instructional leaders should be making many of the crucial decisions about student learning. The implementation of CCSS by individual states and/or school districts could have negative consequences for teachers, and it is impossible to know what will result from the as-yet-undeveloped assessment of the CCSS.

Still, in the best case, the CCSS can offer benefits to teachers. They can make it easier for teachers to deal with transient students by assuring that they have been working toward similar goals in their previous school. The CCSS can provide a lens through which teachers can examine their own practice to find areas that would benefit from more instructional attention or to introduce more balance into the curriculum. A number of teachers have reported that state standards had such effects, and it is reasonable to think that the CCSS might function similarly. Most of all, the CCSS can provide an occasion for teachers to consider what constitutes the most effective ELA teaching.

What is NCTE's stake in the CCSS?

Although it commented on drafts of the CCSS when they were under development, NCTE did not participate in creating these standards. As an association most directly concerned with professional development, NCTE is invested in supporting teachers as they face the challenges posed by the CCSS. In addition, it is an association that values teacher voices, like the ones included in Section II of this volume. To that end, the Executive Committee of NCTE commissioned and invested in the four-volume set to which this book belongs. NCTE is also devoting online resources to providing materials that extend beyond this book and provide a space where communities of teachers can share ideas and strategies.

How should I begin to deal with the CCSS?

As the introduction to this book suggests, it makes sense to begin with students because teachers know more about their students than anyone else. As a first step you might make a list of goals for the students you are teaching now. Consider the skills, dispositions, motivations, habits, and abilities you would like them to develop. Your list probably encompasses every standard in the CCSS along with a good deal more. Keep your entire list in mind as you approach the CCSS, and start by thinking about what your students need to learn.

Looking at the learning needs of students in light of the CCSS can lead, in turn, to considering classroom practices and thinking about how various instructional strategies might be refined or adapted to foster student learning. Looking at classroom practices leads to questions about instructional materials and, ultimately, the curriculum. Woven through all of these is the continuing theme of professional growth and development because asking questions and reconsidering nearly always require changes that are best supported by professional development.

The Common Core State Standards (CCSS) may feel like yet another set of top-down, mandated standards. And integrating the CCSS into the curricula and teaching can, at times, generate feelings of pressure and conflict. But it is also possible to approach the CCSS from a different perspective as well—one that sees opportunities for bridging between good practice based on NCTE principles and policy and what the CCSS offer. The NCTE community, of which this book series is a part, is one space where you can start to build bridges and frame your interactions with the CCSS in ways that are empowering, highlight and encourage best practices in literacy learning, and sustain the incredible work that English teachers are already doing in classrooms. Rather than focusing on how the CCSS will subvert the instruction we are already doing, framing our approach to the standards instead around observing, contextualizing, and building can help us to bridge the CCSS and established instructional practices based on NCTE principles, allowing the two to work in tandem.

First, one way to frame discussions about and approaches to the CCSS is to focus on detailed observation. Before we can become teachers who incorporate these standards in meaningful and pedagogically sound ways into our practices, we need to be learners who observe and take careful note of what exists in the document and what the standards are asking of students. We also need to develop observational lenses through which to see the standards that will keep students and their needs at the center of all instructional change. Learning about the CCSS through close observation may better equip us to advocate for our students' unique needs.

A second way to think about the standards is to use them as a frame for contextualizing. It is important to remember that, while we observe and take note of what exists in the CCSS document itself, we always need to keep specific school and classroom cultures and environments in mind, understanding how different teaching contexts can pose different challenges and opportunities. The teaching vignettes you will read in this section seek to display and honor a variety of school contexts, cultures, and teaching environments, but not all of the teachers in this volume approach planning with the CCSS in the same way, and their lessons don't look the same. A consideration of local context, then, must be coupled with detailed observation of the CCSS document itself.

Third, we can see the CCSS as a frame for building our instruction and classrooms and for meeting students where they are and keeping their needs at the center of lesson design and instruction. To build with the CCSS in mind, we need to begin to see them as more than boxes to check off on a list or forces mandated from above that are seeking to destroy our classrooms. Instead, building *from* and at times *with* the CCSS will involve developing knowledge about the document itself, examining and evaluating our current experiences in the classroom and the culture in which we teach, and relying on the communities around us for support and assistance.

This book, then, is framed around observing the CCSS closely, contextualizing these standards to address specific students in specific schools, and building instruction that integrates the CCSS with NCTE principles for teaching English language arts.

Observing

Detailed observation of the CCSS can begin with identifying where the standards may present shifts from previous state standards documents and identifying patterns in the language of the CCSS document. By looking across the document in this way, you can see some of the most salient shifts. Below, you will find a brief overview of student-focused shifts and instructional shifts that occur in the CCSS document, as well as references to specific CCSS document pages where you can seek greater specificity about these themes.

Student-Focused Shifts

- *Meaning-making*—The CCSS require that students will do more than just read texts for basic comprehension; instead, students will be expected to pull from multiple sources to synthesize diverse texts and ideas, consider multiple points of view, and read across texts. (See, for example, pages 8 and 40 of the CCSS document.)

- *Developing independence*—The ultimate goal of each standard is that all students will demonstrate the ability to enact key skills and strategies articulated in the CCSS on their own. To help students reach this goal, the CCSS spiral expectations across grade levels. Standards for the elementary grades, for example, include language about how students should enact the standard "with support." To clarify, this expectation does not diminish the need to scaffold instruction at all grade levels; rather, the goal is to move students toward independent enactment of standards. (See CCSS document, page 7. Note that while there are times when the language of independence is explicitly stated as on page 55, this expectation is also embedded in assumptions about all CCSS.)

- *Transfer of learning*—On page 7, the CCSS state that students will be required to respond to a variety of literacy demands within their content area courses—ELA *and* others—and to discuss with others how their ability to meet these demands will prepare them for the demands they will face in college and in their future careers.

- *College and career readiness*—Linked to transfer, on page 7, the CCSS expectations articulate a rationale for what college- and career-ready high school students will be able to do. There is little, if any, focus on rote memorization. Rather, the CCSS focus is on skills, strategies, and habits that will enable students to adapt to the rhetorical demands of their future learning and contributions.

Instructional Shifts

It is important to reiterate that the CCSS do not mandate *how* teachers should teach; this is even stated explicitly on page 6 in the document. Why a focus on instructional shifts? Clearly, just as the CCSS spell out what students will be expected to do, the CCSS may prompt shifts in our thinking about how best to help students meet these expectations, which will inevitably affect our teaching.

- *Spiraling instruction*—Unlike some state and district standards, the CCSS do not promote instructional coverage. Instead, the CCSS invite spiraled instruction. Students will be expected to enact particular standards repeatedly within grade-level content area courses *and* across grade levels. In part, this is evident when tracing the lineage of a particular standard to the grade level below and above. Parts of particular CCSS are repeated and built on in subsequent grades. The CCSS are therefore meant to build iteratively. On page 30 of the CCSS document there is a graphic representation of this spiraling idea with regard to language skills, but a similar graphic could just as well be created to illustrate the approach to the other ELA threads as well. For further discussion of spiraling instruction, see Section III of this volume.

- *Integration of ELA threads*—On pages 4 and 47, the CCSS encourage an "integrated model of literacy" whereby ELA threads (e.g., reading and writing) are woven throughout units of study.

- *Inclusion of nonfiction or informational texts*—On page 5, the CCSS set explicit expectations regarding the kinds of texts students read and write. By twelfth grade, 70 percent of the sum of students' reading, for example, is to be informational, nonfiction reading. But as we discuss further in Section III, the responsibility for this reading is shared by all content area teachers. Still, the inclusion of more informational text may present a shift for some.

- *Text complexity*—Page 57 of the CCSS document offers a descriptive graphic on text complexity. NCTE principles affirm the range of ways that strong ELA teachers introduce increasingly complex texts to student readers. These include but are not limited to student interest, genre, language, content, and ELA concepts foregrounded in instruction. For further discussion of text complexity, see Chapter 2 in Section II where Sarah Brown Wessling shares about how she approaches text complexity in relation to the CCSS.

II

Contextualizing

2

Everything's a Conversation: Reading Away Isolation

Meet Sarah Brown Wessling, Johnston High School

In the sections and chapters that follow, I will invite you into my classroom, along with the classrooms of other high school English language arts teachers whose experiences in planning and implementing instruction can help you to think about how you can contextualize and build using the CCSS, established NCTE principles, and the instructional practices you already use that work well.

My teaching began twelve years ago, eleven of which have been at Johnston High School in Johnston, Iowa, where I have taught a range and variety of courses throughout my tenure. The suburban high school, currently comprised of 1,300 students in grades 10 through 12, has seen incredible growth in population over the past fifteen years, which has created a steady trajectory of adding teachers, managing ballooning class sizes, and ever-changing student populations. Each year, this community now welcomes more ELL (English language learner) students and those utilizing free and reduced-price lunch. While some courses at the high school are on a block schedule, all courses in the English department meet once a day for forty-four minutes. All but two course offerings (tenth-grade Integrated Language Arts and Advanced Placement Literature and Composition) are semester length. Students choose classes from a newly reconstructed set of course offerings designed around fifteen thematic topics (e.g., Teen in the World, Power of Persuasion, Reading the Screen, or Culture Clash). Designed around themes, these courses each integrate various strands of literacy—reading, writing, speaking, viewing, and listening—and each position fiction, nonfiction, and informational texts in the context of unit construction. These course offerings are designed for differentiation within each class, so all kinds of learners are included in any given classroom of approximately twenty-three to twenty-eight students. In addition to my work at Johnston High School, I served as a national ambassador for education as the 2010 National Teacher of the Year.

When you walk into my classroom, you'll find a Jackson Pollock print on the wall. At the beginning of the school year it usually doesn't take too long for a student looking at it to say something like, "I could be famous too if all I did was take paint and splatter it all over a canvas." I wait in anticipation for this moment of provocation, when a student unknowingly invites a conversation about the difference between appearance and reality, the relationship between chaos and precision. I'm anxious to tell them about Pollock's immersion into process, his captivation with intentionality and his precision of practice that transcends into art. The work of Jackson Pollock reminds me that like quality instruction, what may appear chaotic is deliberate, precise, and carefully designed.

Contextualizing

The way we design instruction with local context and the CCSS in mind determines the kind of learning that will emerge on the canvas of our classrooms. What we emphasize, what we say, and what we spend our time engaged in will emerge in what and how our students learn. So, we are deliberate, knowing that what happens on the first day and how it connects to the last day matters. We are precise, cognizant that the language of learning permeating our classrooms affects thinking.

In concert with my classroom accounts, co-contributors to this volume, Danielle Lillge and Crystal VanKooten, spent time collaborating in English language arts classrooms and have created companion vignettes that will take us into additional environments that are balancing classroom practice with standards integration. All the teachers in this volume have generously invited us into their classrooms to experience teaching and learning moments that illustrate how the chaos of their classroom life is indeed deliberate, precise, and carefully designed. The teaching and learning practices described highlight the ways these teachers work to enact NCTE principles that affirm the value of the knowledge

As you read through the chapters in this volume, look for the following symbols to signal various themes and practices.

Common Core State Standards

Collaboration

Connections

Integrated Teaching and Learning

Honoring Diversity

and experience students bring to school, the role of equity in literacy learning, and—always—the learning needs of students while attending to the CCSS. Each of two teaching and learning vignettes within each chapter is preceded by a brief description of the context in which the teacher and his or her students are working and is followed by an explanation of the teacher's journey to developing pathways to enact these practices because, as we all know, exemplary moments in teaching are the product of many years of studying classroom practice, discussing ideas with colleagues, and reflecting on teaching and learning. Charts following the vignettes highlight key teaching and learning practices and connect them with specific CCSS and with NCTE research-based principles, and finally, the "Frames That Build" sections offer exercises to help you think about how the teaching and learning practices highlighted in the vignettes can connect to your local teaching context.

Connections

Section III focuses exclusively on the building frame. There, you will find specific resources for building your instruction with the CCSS and for working with colleagues to observe patterns in the CCSS document compared to previous local and state standards.

It is our hope that these teaching and learning vignettes and the corresponding materials will serve as a reflection of the language of learning that already fills your classrooms, and that they will demonstrate a framework that allows thinking about not just *what* we do, but *why* we do it. We hope they will remind us that in the layers of local, state, and national values, the greatest intentionality comes from the classroom teacher who enters the complexity and emerges with a process that honors the learning in our classrooms. We invite you to step into these classrooms, reflect on them, and use their successes and challenges to further your own thinking about what bridges you can build between the CCSS and your own instruction.

Teaching and Learning Practices for Reading: Sarah's Classroom

I remember noticing the time that spring afternoon during my second year of teaching. My ninth graders and I had spent the last forty-five minutes going question for question, point for point, and I had a sinking feeling as I realized this would be our last discussion of Maya Angelou: the posturing of points. Did it really matter if they could recall every *what* I put in front of them? I thought I had been using themes, such as power, to frame this unit, but actually, I was still teaching the details of a book, not offering for my readers the kind of authentic experience we all crave. I was teaching them how to read for school, not for life, and thus, I couldn't blame them for how I'd inadvertently set up this horrible forty-five minutes of point-mongering.

I vowed to rethink what it meant to be an authentic reader, to reread Nancie Atwell and Louise Rosenblatt with the eyes of experience wide open. I paid attention to my own reading habits, especially as I read challenging texts and worked to construct meaning with them. I quickly realized that texts cannot operate in isolation the way I was teaching them. I had been organizing my teaching around themes, but

I hadn't really been using them to prepare students to read for complexity because I still was teaching the *what* of *I Know Why the Caged Bird Sings* without the kind of context and texture that liberates students to read complex texts for layers of meaning.

The shift in how I created reading experiences has its roots in that day. To realize that change, two things had to happen: (1) I needed a shift in thinking and (2) I needed a deliberate and honest implementation of that new paradigm. That day serves as a poignant reminder that there are all kinds of "moves" in our classrooms that quickly, silently, powerfully subvert our best intentions. In this case, using a highly objective test spoke more loudly about what I valued in a reading experience than any mention of our theme had up to that point.

So, my inquiry began in understanding *how* to craft a reading experience that scaffolded us to greater understanding and meaning-making. As I realized that teaching a theme and thematic teaching were distinctly different instructional endeavors, it also occurred to me that teaching thematically meant I had to design reading experiences in such a way that texts would talk to each other. I started by gathering a variety of texts that extended one main text in similar ways. *Romeo and Juliet* was preceded by excerpts of marriage stories from *Marry Me* as well as selected Shakespearean sonnets. Instead of watching a film version of the play, we juxtaposed excerpts of three different versions, working to establish how nuanced interpretations offered texture to our interaction with *Romeo and Juliet*.

Connections
Sarah's use of a thematic approach is one way to organize units. See Section III for more ideas about how to plan with this in mind.

Soon, even this approach gave way to more intentionality in text selection and, thus, more complexity. Later, I recognized that my centerpiece text was never as powerful without the benefit of other texts to provide context. *The Stranger* wasn't as powerful without excerpts of *Sophie's World*, Charlie Chaplin, or punk rock music to amplify it. Our investigation of it wasn't complete without juxtaposing Camus to Jean-Paul Sartre's *No Exit* to offer contrast, to spark questions, to prompt curious distinctions. Before long, we were hearkening back to Salinger, Peter Kuper's graphic novel of *The Metamorphosis*, and *One Flew Over the Cuckoo's Nest*. Even though we moved on to a juxtaposition of Flannery O'Connor and Mary Shelley, our discussion of good and evil was fueled by the likes of Mersault and the other authors, characters, and ideas that permeated our course. I had not only learned to teach thematically, but I had also learned how to design a recursiveness in text selection that mirrored and honored the kind of recursiveness we practiced as writers, thinkers, viewers, and readers.

Sarah's Journey: Pathways to Enact These Practices

A consistent feature in the CCSS, one that extends across all grades, asks students to stop seeing texts as isolated pieces of work and to compare them to other texts. As the texts become more complex and students become more savvy, the reading goes beyond even compare/contrast and moves toward juxtaposing texts to reveal their layers and nuances. Certainly, one component of helping students read complex texts resides in the strategic instructional moves that guide and scaffold students while they are in the process of reading the texts. Yet, as we interpret the CCSS, it's equally important to consider how we select texts and organize reading in a way that invites scaffolding and establishes layered reading of complex texts.

Integrated Teaching and Learning

Sarah's approach to texts resists having students read one text in isolation, but instead seeks to layer different types of texts—print, canonical, multimedia, and popular culture texts—on top of one another.

Reading, especially complex reading, doesn't occur in isolation. In imagining a reading experience that is scaffolded by design, that resists reading in isolation, and welcomes a situation in which texts "talk" to each other, I've used a concept (see Table 2.1) to design instruction that deliberately layers the reading of texts by way of conceptual reading circles (unlike student reading groups, these "circles" demonstrate how we can layer the reading of classroom texts). Just as I started with *Romeo and Juliet* or *The Stranger*, many teachers may begin by choosing their major or *fulcrum* text, the selection that is the centerpiece of any unit of study. The fulcrum text is one that offers distinct layers of meaning and complexity for the reader. It may be of considerable length, it may use nonlinear narrative structure, it may be considered a "classic." This is the fulcrum text because it is the most complex and the work that comes before and after helps to tease out and maneuver its complexities. Students work toward reading independence with these texts.

Context texts	Fulcrum texts	Texture texts
These accessible "anchor" texts create a reservoir of prior knowledge that gives context to the complexity of further reading.	*These texts are often the traditional whole-class text or they take the place of that whole-class text.*	*While these texts often seem to be shorter, it also is effective to juxtapose two major texts to create reading texture.*
Film film excerpts informative pieces news/magazine articles blog radio show podcast short story poetry drama young adult literature brief fiction brief nonfiction graphic novel	book-length fiction book-length nonfiction short story or stories drama poem or series of poems film student selected text whole-class text	film film excerpts informative pieces news/magazine articles blog radio show podcast short story poetry drama young adult literature brief fiction brief nonfiction graphic novel

TABLE 2.1: Sample Texts for Reading Complexity Circles

Crucial at this point is letting go of the idea that our focus is teaching the content of the text rather than skills of reading and thinking. In other words, I don't teach *To Kill a Mockingbird*, I teach "courage," and *To Kill a Mockingbird* is but one of the texts used to explore the idea of courage. Therefore, organizing a reading experience around an idea versus a book title becomes central to including both the *context* and *texture* texts that expand the potential of the reading experience. A *context* text(s) anchors the reading experience by generating prior knowledge while connecting to student interests, motivations, and questions. It is accessible and it creates motivation. It may have teenage protagonists or be particularly brief. It deals with the theme or essential question in succinct or overt ways. It may set up vocabulary or scenarios crucial to the other texts; it anchors thinking.

The *texture* texts, then, are read either in conjunction with the fulcrum text or after it. *Texture* texts do just that: add texture to reading and thinking through their juxtaposition. They may be read both simultaneously and/or after other texts. These texts may contradict another work, may focus in on one aspect of another work, or may illuminate another work in some fashion. These texts are often brief because they may be complex, technical, or appropriate for shared reading. As readers must tease out the implicit nuances of these texts, the opening for use of ongoing and specific textual evidence emerges as part of the classroom discourse. Perhaps most importantly, the fulcrum text from one unit then informs the reading and learning of the next unit. In a curriculum that is ongoing and progressive, the fulcrum text in one unit becomes part of the continuing discourse of the class and, thus, becomes part of the context for upcoming units. Just as *The Stranger* went from a fulcrum text in one unit to providing context for Flannery O'Connor in the next, this model creates a recursiveness in which even the units are no longer in isolation of each other.

Certainly, teachers come to this work of implementing reading standards with text complexity from various circumstances. Few teachers are able to imagine and implement without navigating many levels of school bureaucracy. Regardless of one's teaching situation, creating these kinds of reading experiences is possible.

In looking at Table 2.1, it's crucial to note that text types can quickly move from one column to another. Further, these columns are representative of different types of texts, rather than offering a complete list. In implementing reading complexity circles, it's less important to choose the "right" kind of text for each circle and far more vital to use the selected texts with intentionality. In other words, *how* the texts are used to scaffold the reading experience takes precedence over *which* texts are chosen. The same text could work in each of the three circles. For instance, a short story could be the fulcrum text of a unit, knowing that its purpose there is to spend extended time with the short story, teasing out its many layers. In another scenario, the same short story could be juxtaposed with a book-

Common Core State Standards
Students in Sarah's classroom are given opportunities to read a range of texts—literary and informative—including those from various modes and sources. They read texts of increasing complexity at both their independent and instructional levels. Sarah believes this fosters an environment in which learners can take intellectual risks.

length nonfiction text and serve to provide texture or perspective to the nonfiction. In yet another scenario, the short story could create context for the fulcrum text, a drama. Intentionality and execution of the design depends on using all three circles at any given juncture of a course. Simply envisioning a single text in three ways (the short story as representative of all three) underestimates the power and recursiveness of designing with text complexity in mind.

For example, I recently taught a course in which *The Odyssey* was one of the major texts. I began planning by determining which facets of the content I wanted students to learn. The power of allusion? The importance of metaphor? The theme of journey? I also thought about the skills that students should emerge from this unit with. The ability to read closely? The ability to analyze the literature? The ability to write convincingly about the text? Through this exploration, the essential question emerged: How do physical journeys fuel personal insights? With the question posed and the skills to focus on elevated, the content needed to fuel our inquiry. The fulcrum text, *The Odyssey*, became the text we needed to unpack the most. To frame that text, I chose *Star Wars* and some excerpts from Joseph Campbell as context texts. The context texts allowed us to practice our skills and create a reservoir of language and ideas that enabled readers more access to *The Odyssey*. Then, as we read our fulcrum text, we added the potential for nuanced readings by juxtaposing *The Odyssey* with an NPR piece on veterans and violence along with excerpts from the *Frontline* episode "A Soldier's Heart." By making sure that students saw how these texts weren't isolated, but how knowing one lends depth to another, they were far more prepared to deal with the text complexity before them. Layering instructional design in this way also created ongoing writing and speaking experiences.

As we consider enacting these practices, we each have the reality of our book closets to go to. On opening those doors, some may see an abundance of options, while others may feel constrained by what they see. Regardless of your reality, there is a place to begin. Certainly my journey has been a progressive one. Throughout my teaching experiences, I have found myself in a variety of scenarios that range from working within a fixed curriculum, to reorganizing reading experiences in a flexible curriculum, to imagining and implementing a department set of course offerings where all the classes are organized around themes. Taking the resources you have and organizing them using reading complexity circles (see Figure 2.1) can help you authorize *your* readers.

Working within a Fixed Curriculum

As I started teaching, the curriculum already established by the departments was largely fixed with prescribed readings and sometimes prescribed materials. In cases like this, the process of crafting a reading experience begins with text placement. Which texts are already next to each other in the curriculum? Do they have anything

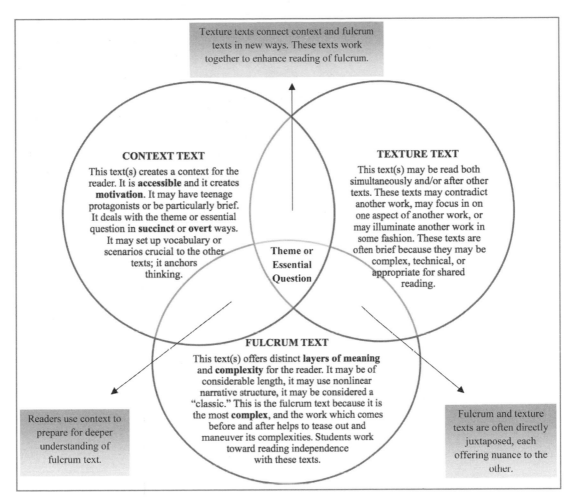

FIGURE 2.1: Reading complexity circles.

to say to each other? Can a few texts that are in close proximity to each other be grouped around a theme or essential question? Which short, accessible texts could I bring into the classroom to provide a context? How will the language of the theme serve as "reading Velcro" for each subsequent text? Often, in a fixed curriculum, the fulcrum text was canonical. Yet even with a traditional text at the center of unit design, I could still consider which texts to bring in from other units. I could also scour classrooms for unused resources that could add texture to the reading, discussion, and analysis of that major text. If you are using a textbook, ask if the selections can be reorganized around a theme or question. Imagine the selections becoming context or texture texts for other selections. Regardless of how tight the constraints on your curriculum may be, organizing study around themes, bringing in short anchor pieces for context, and getting the texts you have out of isolation and into conversation with each other will advance a more authentic reading experience.

**Collaboration**

As Sarah's experience indicates, one place to meaningfully collaborate with colleagues is through the development of a flexible, textured reading curriculum.

Working with a Flexible Curriculum

Several years into my career, as I acquired some experience and demonstrated competence in the classroom, the potential for a more flexible curriculum emerged. I volunteered for curriculum committees and found that I could still meet the local standards while reconfiguring *how* I went about organizing our learning. This flexibility enabled me to collaborate with other teachers in an effort to shift texts from one course or unit to another. In this case, there was the potential to rewrite or write in units of study where context, fulcrum, and texture texts align. In this case, it was helpful for me to reimagine the fulcrum text. Did it have to be the same whole-class novel whose place in the curriculum has seemed cemented? What if the text was nonfiction? What if it was poetry instead of a novel? What if it was contemporary instead of classic, or classic instead of contemporary? What if it was a literature circle or individual choice instead of whole class? In this case, reimagining the role of that major text as a fulcrum invites companionship with other texts where it may have been shadowed before. I also started to look outside of my closet and the department for resources. Could your library, school or public, find enough copies of a graphic novel to use as a texture text? Is there a young adult literature selection in a neighboring grade level that could create a context? Is there another department that uses full-length nonfiction texts that could be juxtaposed with the fulcrum text?

When You Can Create the Curriculum

Most recently, as several influences aligned, my department and I had the opportunity to imagine and create a curriculum with the support of resources and funding. In this unique situation, the possibility of organizing not only units but entire courses around reading circles offered the potential for ongoing scaffolding from text to text, unit to unit, and course to course. As Figure 2.1 shows, reading circles bring multiple texts together.

Beyond Design: Meeting Readers Where They Are

I think that many teachers have long taught to a set of standards. It's that intersection of content and skill all learners must have to be equipped as a member of a highly literate and quickly changing society. While teachers just entering the profession may draw from a defined set of national standards such as the CCSS to help them find focus and purpose in their work, those teachers who have already established an "internal compass" of sorts come to this work of integration with a unique challenge. While established teachers may quickly understand the standards, I have found, through my own efforts and by working with other teachers, it's taxing to determine how the language and implications of the standards make it into our day-to-day work.

Wielding a blueprint of instructional design means we've created the capacity for students to construct their own learning; meeting them in that process comes next. Teaching readers to be thinkers means we must engage with our students as they work to comprehend what they read, to use explicit evidence to support their readings, to pay close attention to word meanings, and to integrate the ideas of several texts to support their own response. The language of the reading standards sends us a clear message: Students must be able to read carefully and closely, using precise evidence to support analysis. This means that we will help students to use their personal connections and responses to texts as entry points, knowing this practice creates access to a text. It also means that as we guide students to reading as a generative process, the way they exit a text may be precipitated on how they entered it, but they will emerge from the reading having attended to precise language and having interacted with its nuances. I often think of the kinds of questions that surround our work in the classroom as either **entry questions** or **exit questions**. In other words, we will ask the kinds of questions that give our students *entrance* into a text: the question that activates schema, that connects to what they know, that piques a personal interest. Once they're "in" we need to ask the kinds of questions that help them *exit* the text with a nuanced, layered reading. When we center our prismed readings on the precise language of the text, we're helping students to explore *how* or *why*.

Common Core State Standards
The CCSS use the language of Anchor Standards (the standards that apply to 6–12) and grade band specific standards, which are delineated into 1a, 1b, and so forth. See Figure 1.1 for further clarification.

So often, when working with standards, we subscribe to the subtext that if we teach all of the discrete parts (the grade band standards and even the further delineated interpretation of those, which often happens at the local level) then students will surely achieve the standard. However, it seems much more likely that if we teach to the anchor standard, and use the language of the grade band standards to inform our feedback and to guide our scaffolding, the purpose and focus of learning remains clear and steady. Otherwise, we operate with a compass that relies on our learners to make the connections and determine the learning purpose by virtue of being the only ones who have "done all of the grade band assignments." It becomes part of our charge to resist a linear approach that compartmentalizes assignments corresponding to grade band standards and offer, instead, a recursive approach that moves in and out of standard and skill, recognizing that we aim to layer them for more authentic purposes rather than stack one task on top of another, hoping it won't all topple over.

One way in which I aim to maintain a larger focus is through naming and enacting a process of reading, of thinking. In the beginning days of class, students talk not about what it means to be a good student, but what it means to be a good learner. As concepts of curiosity, playfulness, divergence, and perseverance enter their vocabulary, the focus of classroom work becomes not just acquiring a content-knowledge base or wielding a set of skills, but also on acquiring the dispositions that make someone an autonomous, lifelong learner.

At the end of every quarter, my students use a taxonomy of these dispositions to trace their progress as learners. Divided into six sections—reader, writer, viewer, communicator, thinker, and habits of mind—this taxonomy then fans out into two more layers. The next layer highlights words that would describe each section followed by a layer that describes the actions embodied by the learner. For example, a reader is also described as "active," "critical," and "voracious." Some of the actions are "recognizing and building on patterns" or "challenging texts and conventional readings." Students gauge their progress by highlighting just a couple of descriptors or actions they demonstrate. Through reflection and documentation, they connect the descriptions to their work and then choose a couple of new descriptors to pursue in the next quarter. This reflective invitation to the students serves as an outward reflection of the implicit process and about what inspires and guides my commitment to students: the belief in their ability to become autonomous, lifelong learners.

As you prepare to meet the teachers of Oak Park in this companion vignette, you'll certainly see this same commitment to student learning reflected in their work. As Danielle Lillge takes you into their classrooms, you'll be privy to how an entire team is establishing a culture of literacy that parallels the deepening reflections and practices of its teachers.

Meet the English Language Arts Team, Oak Park High School

The CCSS guide the work of a team of Oak Park High School ELA teachers including Peter Haun, Carissa Peterson, Ann Rzepka, and Steven Snead, with the help of Linda Denstaedt, who are committed to changing their instruction with the goal of improving student learning. Understanding how and why this team of teachers has come together around the CCSS involves first considering the factors influencing their work.

Having transitioned from a white, Jewish, middle-class community to an urban fringe, black, working- and middle-class community over the past two decades, Oak Park's population shift is further complicated by the effects of economic downturn as families have left the city in search of jobs. Once a high school of 1,800 students, today the high school's 800 students arrive at school each day not only from local Oak Park neighborhoods but also through open-enrollment from nearby Detroit. The loss of student enrollment is also part of a larger narrative about how the school district's $10 million deficit affects the quality of education. One huge indicator of these effects came when only 5 percent of Oak Park High School students demonstrated proficiency on state tests; consequently, Oak Park was labeled a high school in need of improvement.

Further complicating teachers' realities, Oak Park High School is the recent recipient of a large federal Shared Instrumentation Grant (SIG) aimed at funding instructional change that will improve students' performance, achievement, and ultimately test performance. SIG's immediate impact was on the administrative and staff population. This year, under the guidance of a new administrative team, approximately half of the high school's staff members are new to the building; many teachers, including Carissa and Ann, arrived after having taught in the district's middle-level buildings for years. The newly combined Oak Park faculty is charged with improving student performance. Without SIG the school district's deficit would likely prevent the Oak Park ELA team teachers from focusing on essential and complex instructional change. But, SIG also raises the stakes more than ever before; if the Oak Park ELA team members and their colleagues' efforts do not improve student performance, then the school runs the real risk of closure.

At this unique moment in their school's history, the Oak Park ELA team teachers have found in the CCSS a rationale to reshape their instruction and curricula, an impetus to think much more deeply and purposefully about their professional work, and a challenge they are only beginning to tackle with urgency. The CCSS focus on developing students as readers, writers, and thinkers across disciplines is something that has encouraged ELA team members to see their work as culture shifting and shaping. Just as the larger Oak Park community continues to shift, the team teachers recognize the need to help redefine the school culture in support of literacy learning that raises expectations for what students are capable of achieving.

This commitment to redefine school culture that will benefit student learning comes with associated challenges—for students and teachers. One such challenge emerges from generational, socioeconomic, cultural, and racial factors that form disconnects between students and teachers. As one of two African American male teachers in the school, Steven, who also taught in a model Detroit school, notes, "Most of our students come to school and there's no one here like them." Other challenges result from a school culture that has most recently focused on the maintenance of the status quo. As special education and content area teachers collaborate, they face the difficulties of redefined professional roles and disparate training in team-teaching and literacy-based instruction. Additionally, students were not expected to read at home until this year, Carissa explains. And in Ann's sixteenth year of teaching at both the middle school and high school levels, this is the first year that her students have had access to books that they are able to take home from school to read. She shares her colleagues' concerns about changing the school culture from one where "students aren't expected to even play school" to one where students meet "high expectations" because they can with the right instructional support. These are but a few of the challenges the Oak Park ELA team face as they endeavor to shift their practice in support of literacy learning.

Teaching and Learning Practices for Reading in the Oak Park Team's Classrooms

As part of their effort to establish a school culture of literacy, the Oak Park teachers focus their reading instruction on developing students' ability to think about texts more deeply. By articulating and substantiating claims, for example, the learning tasks team teachers ask students to enact are congruent with the CCSS. All four teachers are working with students to understand how to meet such expectations by summarizing main ideas in reading selections, drawing on textual support for claims about the events and elements in the text, and articulating orally and in writing their interpretations of the textual evidence in support of their claims about the reading. However, the fluidity between reading, talking about reading, and writing about reading make extrapolating reading practices from other ELA threads such as speaking and listening difficult in the interactive, discourse-oriented classrooms Oak Park team teachers have established. If you were to walk into the Oak Park ELA team teachers' classrooms, you would find teachers modeling for students the moves, thinking, and talk that critical readers employ within the interactive, discourse-oriented approach they all share. Over time, team members have come to identify the following four elements you will see at play in the classroom snapshots below as central to how they define their interactive, discourse-oriented classrooms: shared habits of mind, skills, and strategies; authentic engagement in classroom talk; common language; and regular instructional adjustments based on student feedback data.

Carissa is modeling for her twelfth-grade students how she records her thinking about reading in her Reader's/Writer's Notebook as part of Oak Park's shared habits. Students *and* teachers keep notebooks where they record their thinking. "Let me

> **Integrated Teaching and Learning**
>
> Most basically, the Oak Park team defines an interactive, discourse-oriented approach as one that views learning as a result of working with, listening to, and contributing to conversations with others through various ELA threads. For these teachers, discourse is the line through which reading, writing, speaking, listening, and therefore learning grow.

show you how I set this up in my notebook," she explains before showing students explicitly how she makes decisions about what to record. Beyond just showing, Carissa expects her students to try on the process she models as "good critical readers"; she believes they are capable contributors to the collective learning in a class where half of the class population includes special education students. Her interactions with students acknowledge their thinking as a valuable asset to the shared learning through discussion: "Good point. I didn't even include this one, Marcus," she says, "Thank you." Her encouragement of student responses also opens space for her to challenge students' thinking: "I have a question for you. How does that quote about the sit-ups support what we said above?"

Seated in small tripods of desks next to large picture windows with walls displaying student work, Peter's eleventh-grade students discuss their reading of *Night*. His students write entries in their Reader's/Writer's Notebooks in preparation for class discussion of characterization in the book. They work quietly but collaboratively in short conversations with others at their tripod about how their interpretations and connections link to one another while Peter canvasses the room writing observations on his clipboard and listening in on students' conversations. Students' purposeful engagement in classroom talk reflects Oak Park team members' efforts to help students

Common Core State Standards
Team members' efforts build on the CCSS shift toward meaning-making as central to reading.

use talk as a way of making meaning of texts. Teachers' help, though, comes not only from direct interaction with students but also from the way that they plan for and facilitate conversation in their classrooms. In the tripod discussions, Peter's students clarify tasks for one another, provide each other with what he calls the "extra boost" to push their thinking further, and enact what strong readers do as they read. Peter's efforts to establish a classroom community where discussion about reading is central results in a classroom dynamic where, he describes, students "get more help from each other than I could possibly" offer.

Across the snow-covered courtyard Steven's tenth-grade students review story elements related to their reading of *The Color Purple*. He encourages students to substantiate the claims they are making about particular characters. At one point he says to Richard, "I like the claim you made. Celie does not know how to stand up for herself. We just need to find the evidence for that." And when another student offers textual evidence by reading from a particular page, Steven presses her to explain the connection between the evidence and the claim: "How does that confirm the claim on the board about Celie?" At the same time, Steven sees value in helping his students understand why this discussion of claims, evidence, and interpretation matters beyond the immediacy of his classroom. He explains how the thinking moves students are making connect with the thinking employers are going to expect of the

Common Core State Standards
Team members' focus on claims, evidence, and interpretation emerges directly from the high school reading standards.

students in the future. Oak Park teachers have committed to a common language as part of their interactive, discourse-oriented approach. All team members are talking with students throughout the building about claims, evidence, and interpretation.

Visitors entering Ann's twelfth-grade English classroom down the hall find charts lining the walls, student desks facing one another, and an inviting area rug at the center of the space. The class is engaged in a discussion of *The Lovely Bones*, and Ann draws their attention to one chart in the center of a blackboard, which says, "Readers learn about characters through the <u>problems</u> they face. Readers use this knowledge to predict what will happen in the end of the novel." As they continue, Ann prompts students to return to the sticky notes they use to record their thinking while reading prior to class discussion. "Yes," she encourages, "so find the exact sentences in your books" that warrant the claims and interpretations drawn about the characters' problems. When Ann invites students to record their interpretations with textual support, she grabs a clipboard from her desk and travels around the room; she checks in with students for brief conferences about the sticky notes they prepared for class before bringing the class back together for a discussion of what they have found.

Integrated Teaching and Learning

Team teachers' charts serve as reminders for students of class discussions and the moves or decisions that strong readers, writers, and thinkers enact.

Connections

In conversations such as Ann's, Oak Park team members are formatively assessing students' ability to engage with the text as they read using data they collect during each lesson both in student work and from classroom talk. Ann speaks about being able to adjust her instruction the following day as necessarily dependent on what she finds. For other ideas about how you might employ formative assessments, see Section III.

The Oak Park Team's Journey: Pathways to Enact These Practices

Past Practice

The use of an interactive, discourse-oriented workshop approach to instruction and learning is new for Oak Park students and most ELA teachers alike. In the past, ELA teachers worked from a common single textbook where they and their students plodded from reading selection to selection, and students had become accustomed to what Carissa describes as "answering question after question" in response. Peter humbly recognizes his reliance on the textbook and associated handouts drew heavily on his "own education." By and large Oak Park students were asked to recount information, follow procedures, and, as Ann describes, "play school."

Shifting Practice

The omnipresent threat of school closure has no doubt motivated team members' efforts to change instruction; yet at the same time, these teachers are deeply committed to providing their students with opportunities for learning that will benefit them beyond their days at Oak Park High School and beyond their experiences with one high-stakes test. In other words, SIG may have prompted the teachers' immediate motivation to shift practice, but their commitment to their students stokes the fire that maintains their energy in the face of this challenging and uncharted journey.

Even so, team members' commitment alone would not sustain their efforts without access to and opportunity to collaboratively learn about instructional practices that best support their students' learning. The team members attribute much of their success in establishing a framework that grounds their instructional conversations and offers a map for their planning around the CCSS to the ongoing, sustained support of literacy leader Linda Denstaedt. Drawing on more than thirty years of classroom teaching, literacy leadership, authorship, and her role as co-director of the local Oakland National Writing Project site, Linda works with the team and other Oak Park teachers regularly in varied capacities. She is eager to attribute the team members' progress to their commitment to shifting and reflecting on their practice. But, as they describe the evolution of their work together where some team members questioned Linda's role early on in the year as "yet another" outsider keen on telling them what to do, the team members now eagerly talk about a synergetic working relationship with Linda. They note that Linda values their expertise and comes to conversations as a colleague; team members explain that her feedback and questions guide their decision making and shape a vision for what is possible at Oak Park High School for students and teachers alike. They believe in what they are creating together and they value Linda's role in helping them to achieve this shared vision.

In collaborative work with Linda and in regular guiding consultation with the CCSS, one key aspect of the team's shifting practice is their adoption of a discourse-oriented, interactive workshop approach to their classroom instruction. But just what this approach will grow to mean is something that the teachers are identifying and considering further as they enact units of study around this instructional model. At this point team members define a discourse-oriented, interactive workshop as one that contains the following elements:

- *Shared habits of mind, skills, and strategies across ELA threads*— Linda talks about developing students' "ways and tools for adopting an academic identity and/or creating metacognition and agency." Among these CCSS informed habits, skills, and strategies are those highlighted in the vignette snapshots in this chapter

 **Collaboration**
The Oak Park team collaborates with the help of Linda. Many schools and districts have literacy coaches who work with groups of teachers. In Appendix A, you will find a list of resources about these types of collaborations.

 **Common Core State Standards**
By drawing much of their common language for describing skills and strategies directly from the CCSS, Oak Park teachers are beginning to see the benefits for students. Peter teaches a resource class that includes students who have different ELA teachers. He talks readily about how these students are able to help one another and talk about what they are doing in different classes, even across grade levels, because they share the same language for naming the work they are engaged in. For Peter, the common language affords him opportunity to support students' learning across courses in ways he might not otherwise be able to.

around summarization, crafting claims, supporting claims with textual evidence, and warranting claims with logical explanations.

- *Authentic engagement in classroom talk*—Team teachers value talk, or discourse, as a critical vehicle for student learning. When students are asked to engage authentically in classroom discourse—whether in writing or speaking—with contributions that evidence their thinking and openness to others' thinking, the Oak Park ELA team teachers have found students' understanding and ability to extend their thinking far surpass the teachers' past experiences of classroom interaction.

- *Common language*—But it's not just about random talking for Oak Park ELA team teachers; rather, their focus on the centrality of language serves two specific purposes. First, team teachers' shared language in their conversation about practice with one another enables them to label and talk concretely about the teaching practices they are enacting. The language they share to describe the pedagogical moves they make helps them translate their instruction into student actions. It is therefore not uncommon to hear team teachers explain to their classes, "Today during your independent reading, I want you to do what I just modeled for you." Second, teachers use a common language with students to name explicitly and make visible the strategies and essential content that supports critical thinking. They use a common language for identifying and talking about the strategies and skills students are expected to use, or enact, in making meaning of the texts students read and discuss with others. Team teachers share this language as a part of building a culture with shared ways of talking about the work students and teachers are equally engaged in.

- *Regular instructional adjustments based on student feedback data*—A shared language and shared practices also help the Oak Park ELA team teachers identify what to look for when assessing their students' ongoing learning through formative assessment practices. In discussions with students during their independent reading, Oak Park ELA team teachers use what Peter refers to as "quick sorts" to formatively assess students' enactments of the day's learning task or strategy. Through observation and brief conversations with students about their work, teachers collect data in their notebooks to chart the patterns they see in students' work. Using these data, they identify which students meet expectations and which students need further support to identify instructional interventions to consider before proceeding or in preparation for the next lesson.

Connections

Ann describes the close relationship she has come to see between class discussion, her conference discussions, and her formative assessment. "A lot of formative assessment is discussion. If I'm walking around [the classroom], I'm trying to notice and look for evidence to support" students' ability to enact the day's CCSS-informed learning task and thinking.

Honoring Diversity

Since the CCSS expect all students to enact the standards and leave up to teachers and schools how best to do so, Oak Park ELA team members create intervention space during independent reading time and through targeted mini-lessons using classroom data so they can better meet the needs of all students in their classrooms.

Evolving Practice

This list of elements that shape the team's use of discourse-oriented, interactive classrooms is not exhaustive. Instead, the team members recognize that as they work to enact more CCSS informed units of study, they are learning to identify which elements of this approach are most critical to their students' learning and their work with one another. The process of learning with and from their students is ongoing.

It would also be unrealistic to assume that the shift to the CCSS and the interactive workshop, discourse-oriented approach has come easily for Oak Park. The approach presents a different way of thinking about how to engage students. Ann shares honestly, "When I started . . . , I was apprehensive. Sometimes I think we do things for classroom management; I always felt like if I didn't give kids something to do while they were reading, they wouldn't read." Giving up control of the classroom is a sentiment echoed by Ann's colleagues when they describe the leap of faith they took in agreeing to adopt a different instructional approach.

The shift in instruction and CCSS expectations for students has not been without struggle either. For students comfortable with questions and answers in response to textbook reading selections, a discourse-oriented approach to learning "pushed [students] beyond their comfort zone," Carissa describes. "The students have really been resistant. It's hard to make the shift and then see them resistant." But the team teachers also recognize that the instructional shift to an interactive classroom means that students are expected to more actively engage in the work of learning; they can no longer be passive consumers who arrive in classrooms to watch Oak Park teachers work.

Realistically, the Oak Park ELA team teachers' collaborative efforts and journey illustrate the tension between frustration and celebration that accompanies difficult instructional change. In terms of celebration, their move beyond a culture that previously supported students' passive engagement has revealed early shifts in their students' attitudes and abilities. Ann describes, "What we're doing now is making kids think more, instead of handing them the study guide and having them give the right or wrong answers." The payoff for Carissa's students has come as they've seen the relevance in the coursework. She describes how one day after an ACT preparation meeting with the junior class, the students returned to class and shared with her, "This is the first time I've learned anything in English." They were able to see the connections between coursework and what they will be expected to perform on the test as well as future learning. Students' recent performance on the ACT predictor PLAN test posted the highest reading scores ever in the district. Ann has noticed similar ability and engagement

Common Core State Standards
The Oak Park teachers believe the CCSS present an opportunity to raise the level of instruction and cognitive demands on students by focusing attention away from prior procedural display. They see the CCSS as offering them a way of making visible the complexities of teaching aimed at developing the independent readers, writers, and thinkers the CCSS document demands.

in her students' interactions in class: "I'm finding more now that my students are enjoying the book more. I had other teachers complain to me about students who are reading their books in the other teachers' classes."

Charting the Practices

As Danielle has observed and articulated in the Oak Park vignette, how we think and talk about learning speaks volumes about what we value. And we, the teachers in these vignettes, jointly value fostering students' lifelong learning. As Ann, Carissa, Peter, Steven, Linda, and I illuminate a range of pathways by which teachers plan with this goal in mind, we would be negligent if we represented planning as a recipe with the same steps for all. In fact, our individual planning processes vary widely across time, courses, and students. Figure 2.2 represents the range of pathways, or processes, by which teachers consider the integration of their teaching and the learning they plan for students.

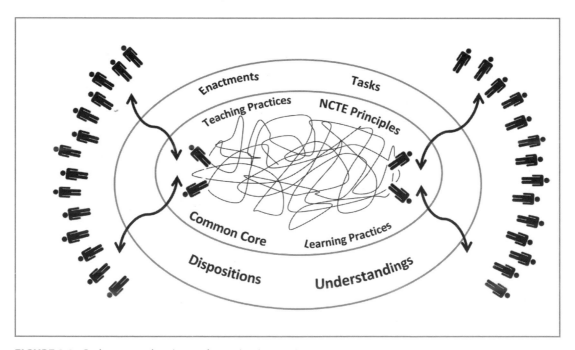

FIGURE 2.2: Pathways to planning and enacting instruction.

Through reflection or conversation, all the teachers in these vignettes speak to some form of wrestling with chaos in describing their thinking about planning. Figure 2.2 represents the chaos that we all navigate, but it also seeks to honor the fact that how we enter this chaos—the pathways by which we get there—varies. Some teachers enter through knowledge about their students, which are represented in the figure as encompassing and informing our thinking. Some teachers enter by thinking about the ultimate goals they have for their students; these are represented in the language of the outer circle including the dispositions, understandings, tasks, and enactments teachers expect students to demonstrate or develop. No matter the entrance, once in the middle we ultimately navigate the chaos that involves considering importantly the meeting place and relationship between these goals and the Common Core, NCTE principles, our teaching practices, and the learning practices we personally develop as well as those we foster in our students. My experiences as well as the vignette teachers' narratives affirm that we meet these considerations through various pathways differently over time.

Figure 2.2 visually represents the way we conceptualize these inextricably linked considerations that are at the heart of our decision making as teachers. We intentionally chose not to represent them as linear and one of our earliest versions of this figure actually included the words in the inner circle embedded within the chaos of the nest at the middle. Given the difficulty of actually reading this chaos, we chose in favor of readability; however, the original visual may more accurately represent why at times it is difficult for us to articulate the complexity of our thinking, acting, and ongoing learning about how to work with and meet the needs of diverse learners. Still, we believe it is possible and quite critical that we work to identify our decision making as well as how we conceive of the elements that inform our decisions, especially as we remind ourselves and others that the CCSS do not dictate the path we choose.

We hope that you will keep Figure 2.2 in mind as you read the charts that follow and that you will find at the end of each vignette chapter. In these charts, we endeavor to represent how the instructional decisions that emerge out of the chaos are, as I mentioned at the start of this section, deliberate, precise, and careful. For ease of representation, these charts read more linearly than the processes they depict. But they include the elements of our decision making and acting out of the chaos and toward deliberate goals and outcomes. Therefore our movement toward the CCSS is informed by the NCTE principles about what makes for strong ELA instruction and learning. With these principles in mind, we enact teaching practices that invite students to enact learning practices that will enable them to meet CCSS. The relationship between teaching and learning practices is key.

Our teaching opens the space and makes explicit for students how they can learn to enact particular tasks and to ultimately take on particular dispositions toward lifelong learning.

Therefore, the following charts highlight some of the key NCTE principles about and teaching practices for reading instruction that the teachers in this chapter's vignettes enact, connecting these to specific Reading Anchor Standards in the CCSS document, and merging how teachers expect students to evidence their ability to enact the standards in their learning.

Common Core Anchor Reading Standards that intersect with these practices (CCSS, p. 35)

Key Ideas and Details
2. Determine central ideas or themes of a text and analyze their development; summarize the key supporting details and ideas.
Integration of Knowledge and Ideas
9. Analyze how two or more texts address similar themes or topics in order to build knowledge or to compare the approaches the authors take.
Range of Reading and Level of Text Complexity
10. Read and comprehend complex literary and informational texts independently and proficiently.

How Sarah enacts the practice ↓	← Teaching Practice →	How Oak Park teachers enact the practice ↓
→ Rotates between individual response, small-group processing and large-group discussion, creating multiple opportunities for students to engage through conversation and writing with multiple fulcrum, context, and texture texts. → Uses the framework of themes and essential questions, creating discourse that relies on varying perspectives.	Establish frames for productive classroom discourse that open opportunities for students to make meaning of texts through conversation with others (e.g., classmates, teacher, those outside of the classroom).	→ Orienting classroom instruction toward classroom discourse and discussion about a range of reading selections. → Employing grouping strategies to facilitate ongoing conversations about texts.
How Sarah's students enact the practice ↓	← **Learning Practice** →	**How Oak Park students enact the practice** ↓
→ Through careful observation, locating patterns, and drawing conclusions, students talk and write in response to texts, working to create nuanced readings.	Students engage regularly in sustained discussion in small and large groups about the texts they are reading and the relationship and connections between texts.	→ Discussing ideas and responses to texts with classmates in small groups and whole-class settings. → Listening and responding to classmates' ideas.

NCTE Principles Regarding Reading
Reading is a complex and purposeful sociocultural, cognitive, and linguistic process in which readers simultaneously use their knowledge of spoken and written language, their knowledge of the topic of the text, and their knowledge of their culture to construct meaning with text.

See pages 120–121 for more on NCTE principles regarding reading instruction.

Common Core Anchor Reading Standards that intersect with these practices (p. 35)

Key Ideas and Details
1. Read closely to determine what the text says explicitly and to make logical inferences from it; cite specific textual evidence when writing or speaking to support conclusions drawn from a text.
3. Analyze how and why individuals, events, and ideas develop and interact over the course of a text.
Craft and Structure
5. Analyze the structure of texts, including how specific sentences, paragraphs, and larger portions of the text (e.g., a section, chapter, scene, or stanza) relate to each other and the whole.

How Sarah enacts the practice	◄——Teaching Practice——►	How Oak Park teachers enact the practice
→ Using a combination of teacher and student choice, texts for students to read are based on how the text will support students' thinking about the texts and themes. → Focusing on varied readings with textual evidence, texts are used to grow students' proficiency as readers capable of making meaning of complex texts.	Create opportunities for students to read for pleasure and to think critically about how and why texts develop, convey ideas, and impact readers as well as how authors craft texts for specific audiences and purposes.	→ Using instructional tools (e.g., sticky notes and charts) to record thinking about reading. → Focusing on varied readings with textual evidence.

How Sarah's students enact the practice	◄——Learning Practice——►	How Oak Park students enact the practice
→ Through relevance to student questions and motivations, learners work toward generating readings that demonstrate nuance, perspective, and a range of ideas.	Students read texts both for pleasure and to think critically about how and why texts develop ideas, convey ideas, impact readers, and reflect a range of author choices.	→ Identifying key ideas in a text. → Drawing on textual evidence to support claims about texts. → Analyzing how and why authors craft texts to develop ideas.

NCTE Principles Regarding Reading
Readers read for different purposes.
The writer's language and knowledge of the topic as well as skill in using written language influence the reader's ability to construct meaning.

See pages 120–121 for more on NCTE principles regarding reading instruction.

Frames That Build: Exercises to Interpret the CCSS

The following exercises may be used by individuals or teams of teachers who are interested in working through the standards. As you unpack the standards, the vignettes may provide a lens through which to view your own individualized implementation of the standards.

- *Reading the standards.* Read the reading standards, looking for the verbs. What is it that students should be able to do as they read? What patterns do you notice in these verbs? Do they coalesce into dispositions for thinking?

- *Looking at text exemplars and sample performance tasks.* Download Appendix B of the CCSS, Text Exemplars and Sample Performance Tasks, and look at a few of the sample performance tasks (pp. 122–123). What do you notice about how the questions are written? What kinds of skills do the questions focus on? What about the questions resonates with the language of the standards?

- *Weighing classroom decisions.* Considering your inquiry into the standards and corresponding exemplars, what implications to classroom practices emerge? Which skills would you elevate for the different texts you read? What language would make it into your assessment tools? How might a focus on concepts versus topics inform your instructional design?

3

Using Viewing to Elicit Complex Thinking

Teaching and Learning Practices for Viewing: Sarah's Classroom

A recurring attribute in the CCSS puts forth the necessity of having students engage with multimedia texts in critical ways. Our students are saturated with visual images. My six-year-old son was surprised to discover that *Harry Potter* was actually a book before it was a movie. My high school students are certain that watching is easier than reading. Perhaps they're right. At least, the way they generally view *is* easier than the way they generally read; the two activities both clamor for more vigor. Teaching visual literacy is crucial to helping our learners make the shift from passivity to activity. Too often our students consume visual media without exploring or deconstructing it. That urge to consume often seems to transfer to the attitudes students have toward a text they read: they want to quickly consume it, perhaps feel it, but they are hesitant to carefully consider it. If we are to alter the habits of our readers, we must then alter the habits of our viewers. If we are to develop thinkers, we need to meet our learners where they are: at the screen. It was this realization that prompted me to think about teaching careful reading differently to my seniors in Advanced Placement Literature and Composition several years ago. Instead of consistently pointing out what they *weren't* doing with the printed page, I wanted to show them what they *could* do with a visual medium and then lead them to *transfer* those skills back to the page. Thus, our unit of careful reading, thoughtful discussion, and meaningful construction began.

Honoring Diversity

While Sarah crafts her film unit within an AP Literature course, film and other visual media can be useful texts for students at any level of study, inviting students with varied abilities and interests to participate in meaning-making through audio and visual modes of expression.

This vignette highlights one of the two ways that film appears in my classes: as a focused study of the genre. Although this vignette will highlight a unit of film study, it's equally important to realize that visual media is part of the fabric of our course. In general, my students lack confidence in their abilities to unpack the layers of the complex texts that come before them. Some students are still resistant to the notion that there *are* even layers to unpack. Yet, if students can't find their place in a process of reading, of writing, of thinking, they won't authorize their own learning. To nudge students toward greater understanding, this portion of a larger unit centered on the individual, society, and the system uses film as a vehicle to explicate the process we've used to explore prose, poetry, and nonfiction.

This experience begins with a letter and a choice. Our school district maintains a policy that all parents must be informed before any full-length film is shown in class, so I use this letter as an opportunity to provide a rationale for visual literacy accompanied by a brief summary of the five film choices students will be able to choose from. Following brief "film talks" the next day, I ask students to rank their top three preferences from these choices: *Searching for Bobby Fischer, Edward Scissorhands, Finding Forrester, One Flew Over the Cuckoo's Nest,* and *The Cider House Rules.* As I work to formulate groups over the next couple of days based on the students' selections, we practice critical viewing strategies during class. Beginning with still shots and key vocabulary terms drawn from John Golden (2001), we develop a common language for discussing what we see. Once we've established confidence with the still shots, we transfer our skills to moving images as we watch television and film clips. Soon, we're ready to begin working with a complete, albeit brief, narrative: the film trailer. This succinct narrative (almost always under two minutes and oftentimes as short as thirty seconds) offers a variety of uses in practicing and illustrating the power of visual images on viewers: (1) viewing and re-viewing the trailer several times in just a few minutes to remind students of the importance of repetition; (2) showing several trailers of the same film to explore how different techniques are used to target different audiences; (3) watching the trailer without the sound, paying attention only to the images; (4) separately, listening to the trailer and then adding the images to discern the impact of the two senses together; (5) scaffolding the practice using Doug Fisher and Nancy Frey's gradual release of responsibility (I do it, we do it, you do it together, you do it alone). In the course of one or two class periods, students can engage with many short texts, which allows them to experience their own viewing and thinking process as it emerges and gains confidence. While in-class practice continues, outside of class, students

Honoring Diversity

Sarah groups students in a variety of ways throughout the course. Sometimes groups are entirely self-selected, while other times she coordinates the groups. This preference method is an effective way to give students choice while still allowing Sarah some latitude in putting together groups that can build on the strengths of all the members. This also allows students to "opt out" of films that may have mature language or subject matter.

Common Core State Standards

Re-viewing the film is crucial because it creates the nuance of watching for different reasons, thus learning to unpack the various layers to synthesize a more complete reading of the trailer's narrative. Looking for specific uses of camera angles or lighting, paying attention to music, or watching for the pacing of cuts can all contribute to the trailer's narrative and effect. Further, this work is a wonderful entry point into the CCSS Reading Standards for Craft and Structure.

 **Collaboration**

Technology can be used as a tool to enable students to work together, and it can be as high-tech or low-tech as the teacher prefers. At a minimum, student groups need access to the film in a way they can pause, go forward, and go backward efficiently. Whether it's using viewing labs in a library or the corners of a classroom, groups need time and space to wrestle with the text.

watch their film for the first time, making observations about cinematic, theatrical, and literary elements while also offering a personal response.

For the next week and a half, our class moves to a section of the library where I have converted study rooms into viewing labs. The student groups (which are generally comprised of three to four members, meaning that often more than one group is studying the same film) then begin their weeklong process of observation, discussion, and analysis as they learn to read the screen. In an effort to be able to work with each group individually at different points in their process, I outline a series of viewing tasks on the first day that the group should manage throughout the week. Doing this allows me to work with groups and students as needed, knowing that because not everyone is in the same place at the same time, I *can* be "everywhere at once." In each step of the re-viewing sequence, students use the viewing labs to re-watch portions of the film again, looking for details, patterns, and layers of meaning. Interspersed in the sequence are conversations with the teacher. This, coupled with the ongoing peer discussions, elicits an opportunity for students to not only work together toward a common goal of uncovering layers of meaning in the film, but it also provides the scaffolding opportunity I need to formatively assess and nudge learners to construct their own learning. Over the week, groups work collaboratively to build into their analysis specific evidence taken directly from cinematic, theatrical, or literary elements of the film. As students engage in detailed re-viewing, they are also preparing for the final component to this unit of study: creating their own film trailer, which argues for their reading of the text (film) using a literary theory. In other words, the groups, which have been working collectively, now determine individual courses of inquiry. If one student chooses to do a psychoanalytic reading of *One Flew Over the Cuckoo's Nest*, then another student may choose a feminist reading, another a Marxist reading, and so on. Because we have already worked with literary theories earlier in the semester, this is a natural extension and application of that work.

Honoring Diversity

As an alternative to storyboards, students could use simple video editing software to create their own trailers or short films that incorporate still and moving images, audio tracks, and written text. Many desktop and laptop computers now come with video editing software already installed.

Some students begin by composing a thesis, a focused idea to guide an argument, and then deductively work to find evidence from the film to support it. Other students are more inductive and collect scenes that they think align with one of what Deborah Appleman (2008) terms as literary "lenses" and then formulate their theses from the collected scenes. Then, instead of composing a formal essay, students create the storyboards for their own film trailer that would argue for their reading of the film based on the chosen literary theory. The storyboards provide a crucial function in that each shot must be accompanied by a description of *what* it is and *how* it creates an intended effect. The students continue to juggle other in-class work, while they have time outside of class to work on their storyboards. This extended work time allows for students to "incubate" their ideas and to use formative feedback as an opportunity to go beyond revision and incorporate rethinking. On presentation day, authors exchange their storyboards with other students, first covering up their intended argument. As readers finish, they determine the intended argument of the trailer based on the shots and intended effects before returning it to the author. This process can be a quick indication of how clearly and effectively the film trailer was composed. Garnering such feedback poises students for, perhaps, the most important move in the design of this unit: thinking metacognitively about the viewing, thinking, composing process.

I begin by asking students to describe their learning process for this project, focusing on any steps they took to reach their final product. As we discuss, students reveal that they "watched the entire film probably five times" or that they "watched the same scene maybe fifteen times" in an effort to be a careful observer and to recognize meaningful patterns. They note how they used the expertise of other group members or how they took a teacher/student conference to rethink their work. They tell how it took them a long time to come up with an idea for their trailer, and that sometimes it took days to determine what the real purpose was going to be. Among other details, they share how carefully they had to think about their audience as they formulated each shot of the storyboard. Without realizing it, the students have described the cognitively complex process of

Common Core State Standards
This kind of metacognitive reflection is one way for students to demonstrate movement toward becoming more independent learners as required by the CCSS. Reflection can also happen through composing written reflections over process, conferencing with the teacher, or talking orally in pairs or small groups.

reading, composing, thinking. I go to the top of our compiled list and replace "Steps Toward Creating a Film Trailer" with "Steps for Reading/Steps for Writing Literary Analysis" and ask the class to put a check by any steps they incorporate when reading a complex text or composing a literary analysis. Most realize immediately that they may have never read a book more than once or pored over a single passage until they could wrap their minds around it. Few spent days looking for a "thesis" and instead relied on sitting down to the computer the night before a paper was due and waiting for it to "just come." When prompted to look at the "intended effect" component of each storyboard, students recognized how carefully they considered the effect of choices such as lighting, angle, sound, or type of cut on the audience. Conversely, students quickly realized how passively they consider the impact of words, punctuation, and sentence structures on readers in the essays they write. By meeting students at the screen, I could help them recognize and employ the kind of complex process that feeds all facets of literacy: reading, writing, speaking, language, *and* viewing.

Sarah's Journey: Pathways to Enact These Practices

In designing this unit, I was deliberate and purposeful in my efforts to foster the habits of mind that characterize learners of literacy who have a tolerance for ambiguity, who challenge comfort zones, who are metacognitive, who are in curious pursuit. As the students progress through the unit, these dispositions are manifested in their questions, revisions, discussions, and constructions. Their productivity can be attributed to both happenstance and design. I had originally created the various steps for student groups to work through at their own pace because we didn't have a viewing lab for every group. However, I quickly recognized that I had inadvertently set up an effective system for me to "be everywhere at once." I quickly noticed that groups needed time to practice without the teacher and with each other. The viewing lab tasks offered just such an opportunity. The tasks required a cognitive complexity that compelled students to go beyond hunting for a right answer and to construct meaning *together*. Additionally, I watched as my "on demand" or "just in time" conferences provided the necessary scaffolding at the right time for any given group. Further, the students worked throughout the entire process receiving all kinds of feedback, but never receiving a grade. Taking grades out of the equation put all the focus on the cognitive task and allowed—welcomed—mistakes as part of a process that was collectively supported by the culture of the classroom. Without assigning group roles, without grades, without worry of mistake, students were liberated to play with observation, to wonder about patterns, to speculate about analysis.

Another facet of the design fostered incredibly collaborative and productive group work: using different literary theories to interpret the same film. This one decision—to not duplicate the use of literary theories in any given group—created a real spirit of collaboration. Throughout the first week and a half of the process, any given group had created a cadre of experts on this one film, this one text. Then, as students started to work on their individual film trailers, each student had access to other experts on the film, on the *content*, to help inform their personal *interpretation*. So often, when a group has the same task, one or two students take over and the others feign ownership. Conversely, when everyone in the classroom has a different task (e.g., all writing a different research paper) peer feedback can be superficial because there is a lack of content expertise. I walked into this model of group content and individual skill quite by accident, but now I work to replicate it as often as possible in my teaching.

Enacting this kind of learning experience certainly meant that I was letting go of the front of the classroom. Creating lab space, opting for students to set their own pace, providing "on demand" feedback, and using class time for *reading* the screen and deconstructing metacognition all contributed to empowering students to come to terms with their own learning process.

In the next vignette, Crystal VanKooten will take you into Steve Bodnar's English classroom. While the film trailer vignette works to further the presence of visual media in our interpretation of the standards, the following vignette prompts us to remember how drama, too, creates the kind of interaction that allows students to construct new meanings.

Meet Steve Bodnar, Southfield-Lathrup High School

Steve Bodnar teaches Senior Composition and Literature at Southfield-Lathrup High School in Southfield, Michigan, a northern suburb of Detroit. Steve has been teaching at the secondary level for fourteen years, and he is and has been involved in the Southfield-Lathrup community in myriad ways: as an advisor for the yearbook, the chess club, and the creative writing club; as the debate coach; as a teachers' union representative; and as a coach for the girls' golf team. The 2010–11 school year has brought new challenges to Steve and his classroom. Because of restructuring in the district due to money constraints and cutbacks, Steve now teaches more students than ever before with five extremely full sections of Senior Comp/Lit daily. Steve's students live in the surrounding middle-class community, but they come from all over the world. Most of the student body is African American (93 percent), but there are also some Chaldean, Jewish, Russian, and African students, along with students who speak English as a second language. Steve's class, Senior Composition and Literature, is a required class that all seniors at Southfield-Lathrup have to pass to graduate. The class focuses on both reading and writing, a large task that engenders both richness and challenges.

Teaching and Learning Practices for Viewing in Steve's Classroom

Two days before winter break, Steve and his Senior Comp/Lit students experienced the first scene of Shakespeare's *Macbeth* together, but not in an expected, traditional way. Steve organizes this unit and its activities using the theme of *perspective*, having students think about, discuss, and apply questions surrounding this theme throughout their study of the play. On this first day, students interact with scene 1 in multiple ways: through reading it silently and aloud, through using the language of the scene to create their own poetry, through watching the scene being performed, through seeing and hearing visuals and music that represent the setting of the scene, and through thinking about thematic elements, including *perspective,* that are present in the scene.

 Common Core State Standards
While this unit does focus on viewing practices, Steve also weaves reading, composition, listening, thinking, and discussion into his lesson, illustrating the integrated model of literacy instruction espoused by the CCSS.

Steve created this lesson with two goals in mind. The first was to set up the events in the opening scene of the play in an understandable, interesting way that would attract and hold the attention of students. To this end, Steve states that he wanted to make the lesson as visual and accessible as possible, enabling his students not just to listen but also to physically participate, look, and touch along the way. Steve's second goal involved emphasizing the theme of perspective in *Macbeth* using the line "fair is foul and foul is fair" as a starting place. He wanted his students to walk away from the lesson familiar with the idea that things in life are relative and that perspective changes depending on how you look at things, a theme central to the events in *Macbeth*. For Steve, these two goals complement one another and enable students to encounter material in new ways that move beyond "sitting at your desk listening to what the teacher says." Instead, his methods encourage the interactive and the visual.

Steve begins his *Macbeth* lesson by handing out printed copies of the first scene to students. The scene is short—the text is less than a page—and the class first reads the scene silently while looking for words that are unfamiliar. Steve asks the class to state aloud the words they don't recognize. Students shout out words such as *hurly-burly*, *anon*, and *heath*. The class discusses what these words mean, and Steve offers his thoughts, as well. Then, the class reads the scene again, this time aloud with volunteers reading the parts of the three witches. After this second reading, there is more discussion about certain terms and what they mean. Then, Steve introduces the blackout poetry activity, an exercise Steve discovered in the work of Austin Kleon. The word *fair* or the word *foul* is written on the top of each student's sheet, and students are instructed to "black out" or cross out words in the scene to form a poem that can be considered either "fair" or "foul." As students begin blacking out words, questions arise. One student asks, "What if your definition of bad is different from everyone else's?" Another comments that the choice of foul words or fair words is really based on the context of the scene. As they black out words and create their poems, students visually see how the omission or inclusion of certain words leads to a particular perspective of reading, and language is made more visible through the activity.

As students continue to cross out words and create their blackout poems, suddenly the lights in the classroom begin to flash on and off, on and off. "Where does this scene take place?" Steve asks the students as he flips the light-switch. "What's the weather like?" As the students respond—"A heath! A storm!"—ominous-sounding music swells through the classroom, and video footage of a lightning storm begins to play on the screen in the front. Through these visual and aural experiences, students are whisked away into the setting of the scene as they complete their poems. After the "storm" subsides, Steve asks students to share their blackout poems if desired with the class, and several students read theirs aloud. After the students share, Steve shares his own blackout poems with the class on the overhead, reading aloud and visually displaying his own interpretations for students.

The next piece of this lesson occurs as students watch the first scene of *Macbeth* performed by professional actors on video. This viewing gives students yet another visual reference point for making meaning with the scene. After the viewing, which lasts only a few minutes, Steve prompts students again to make connections between their blackout poems, the language they heard and saw performed in the scene, and the theme of perspective. He asks students to point out additional lines that represent this theme, and the students point out the line "the battle is lost and won." The class then discusses how a battle can be both lost and won at the same time, and students offer their thoughts: "you might win the battle, but you lost a friend" or "you could lose your mind in the process." Steve then brings it back to the theme: "What's the p word that Kyle said earlier? Perspective!"

Next, the students physically experience a change in perspective as Steve hands out goggles that cause the user to see everything skewed off to the left or right. Students take turns wearing the goggles as Steve asks the students to shake his hand or catch a soft ball. The students have problems doing either of these simple tasks with the goggles on, and the class laughs as they watch the attempts. Steve asks each student with the goggles on to explain to the class what they see and how the goggles change his or her perspective on reality. This activity provides yet another visualization for students of how perspective can change depending on circumstances.

Honoring Diversity

Steve asks his students to move between diverse modes of expression as they explore the theme of perspective from multiple angles: linguistic, visual, audio, gestural, and multimodal. This approach makes content more accessible to learners with different strengths, weaknesses, and abilities.

All of the activities in this lesson help Steve's students visualize, think about, and interrogate the theme of perspective in *Macbeth* from multiple angles. He wants them, above all, to walk away with the idea that things are relative depending on point of view, that "how you look at a situation determines how that situation is." This theme is evident in scene 1 of *Macbeth* and throughout the entire play. Steve states that this kind of thematic learning goal can be realized in interactive, visual ways like those involved in this lesson.

Steve's Journey: Pathways to Enact These Practices

Steve's approach to planning lessons with standards is to incorporate the standards into lessons designed first with students in mind. He explains, "I try to come up with a lesson that I think will be interesting for students. Then I'll sit down and say, which standards am I covering, which should I be covering that I'm not covering?" Steve plans his lessons with his students in mind first because he sees meeting their needs as the sole purpose of his profession: "I see part of my job as trying to get the kids that aren't interested to be interested. The whole point is to help the kids, that's the whole reason I do it. You have to continue to try new things, to be comfortable with what you're doing, and to try to reach as many kids as possible. That's the sole purpose of what I do. I'll do it any way I can." In this way, Steve places a focus

Common Core State Standards

Steve's approach to planning lessons with the CCSS involves keeping students at the center first, then looking at standards second.

on students and their learning first, at the same time emphasizing standards through lessons along the way.

Online Resources

Many districts put on workshops and training sessions similar to the summer institute that Steve attended. In addition, NCTE offers several professional development opportunities, such as its Annual Convention, that can facilitate teacher training and collaboration. For more information, please visit www.ncte.org/books /supp-students-9-12.

The idea for Steve's (Re)Seeing *Macbeth* lesson was born at a "Summer Reading and Thinking Institute" offered through Oakland County Schools that Steve attended in August 2010. This voluntary workshop included teachers from across Oakland County in Michigan, and it enabled Steve to devote time to developing this lesson with attention to visual literacies in particular. At the workshop, Steve practiced an early form of this lesson for colleagues. Steve still meets once a month with a group of teachers who attended this workshop to talk about issues relating to their students' literacy learning. In fact, the development and refinement of this lesson isn't over; Steve's (Re)Seeing *Macbeth* lesson was the subject of a recent group meeting. Steve explains that this opportunity for collaboration with colleagues and reflective practice "keeps me focused and keeps my head in the game" with regard to placing students at the center of practice and instruction and offering the opportunity to continually revise and revisit his lesson plans.

Another benefit of the summer workshop in which Steve participated was that it enabled him to become familiar with the educational theory behind practices such as including more visual literacies into his teaching, such as the work of Freebody and Luke (1990). He states that because of the workshop, he is grounded in a wealth of information drawn from work such as Pahl and Roswell (2005) and Patel Stevens and Bean (2007) about learning styles and visual literacies. He explains, "Now there's the theory behind the actual practice. Why is this going to work? I like knowing why. The workshop I took this summer was my attempt to get that theory behind what I've been doing for several years now." Steve's blackout poetry activity allows students to play visually with printed words as they black out, keep, and rearrange words on the paper in front of them. Students read critically, visualize the shape and meaning of words, and in doing so, compose their own poems. As Steve learned through the workshop and through his developing teaching practices, classroom activities like this one that honor visual modes of meaning-making make space for students to connect with material in new ways and allow students with diverse learning styles to more fully participate in the classroom. Highlighting visual literacies also provides for all students meaningful and relevant connections to traditional reading and writing practices that take place with words.

In addition to collaboration with colleagues and establishing a theoretical base for his practice, Steve also mentions the value of personal reflection and revision in his teaching. Because Steve teaches the same lesson to multiple sections of students daily, he often changes his lessons throughout the day as he sees what works and what doesn't. For example, one change he made was in the way he asked students to create the poems: "In the first hour, the directions were to black out words to keep negative or positive ones in there. Later, the directions were to actually make a poem. I wanted to see if the students came up with something different. I changed it because I thought some students would understand better what I meant." Another change that Steve made to this lesson as the day progressed was to play the storm footage and music as the students read the scene aloud to create a more integrated experience, viewing and hearing the context while reading the words on the page. Steve notes that he makes changes like these often and quickly throughout his day. He constantly asks himself, "Did that work? Why didn't that work? Then I'll try to make a change if I can." This kind of reflective, flexible practice allows for lessons to be continually revised and improved even as they are being implemented.

One way that Steve assesses the learning of his students through a lesson like this one is to review the material in subsequent class periods and see what students remember. Another way that he assesses learning is to see if the students can relate and transfer the theme discussed in the opening scene to new scenes as they move through the play. He performs these assessments throughout the unit as he listens to students' oral responses in class and reads students' written responses in their journal, or at the end of the unit through an assignment such as composing an analysis paper. One such assignment asked students to "read" several of the textbook pictures and to relate their reading to the play by explaining or analyzing what was seen, including finding a quote that went with the picture. Steve comments that his students did an amazing job with this writing assignment. The line that students used much more than any other was "Fair is foul and foul is fair," and Steve argues that the opening lesson using visual imagery had something to do with that. Steve also explains why he doesn't use multiple-choice tests to assess learning: "I don't feel comfortable assessing that way. It's something I never did or wanted to do in my classroom. I didn't see that as really learning. The assessments will be more like pieces of writing, verbal questions, acting out of scenes, and journal entries." The assessments he describes are more varied than traditional multiple-choice tests, and they lend themselves to continuous and formative assessment practices that occur throughout the learning process and not just at its conclusion. Steve's assessments also prepare students for summative evaluation at the end of a unit or at the end of the course through asking students to synthesize material and cultivate habits of mind that will help them negotiate multiple rhetorical and communicative situations in the future.

> **Integrated Teaching and Learning**
> Students look, view, and see in multiple ways throughout this lesson as they visually manipulate words, view and discuss the performances of classmates and professional actors, watch footage of the storm, and observe how a simple device such as goggles can alter perspective. These visual activities occur along with processes of critical reading, writing, speaking, and listening, and students discuss, analyze, integrate, and synthesize information.

Charting the Practices

Both of these vignettes illustrate how class lessons that work well include an inter-twining of all literacy strands—reading, writing, speaking, listening, language, and viewing. Specifically, however, our two vignettes function as powerful examples of the importance of helping students develop visual literacies along with more tradi-tional literacy practices such as reading and writing the printed word. The following charts offer NCTE principles and teaching practices that relate to visual literacies and are embedded in our teaching, connecting these to specific Reading Standards in the CCSS document. *Reading*, in this sense, applies to the ways students learn to view and interpret both written and visual texts such as a film clip or a storyboard. The chart also includes the learning practices students are expected to exhibit in response to the teaching practices.

Common Core Anchor Reading Standards that intersect with these practices (CCSS, p. 35)

Key Ideas and Details
2. Determine central ideas or themes of a text and analyze their development; summarize the key supporting details and ideas.
Integration of Knowledge and Ideas
7. Integrate and evaluate content presented in diverse formats and media, including visually and quantitatively, as well as in words.

How Sarah enacts the practice ↓	← Teaching Practice →	How Steve enacts the practice ↓
→ Crafts viewing experiences in which student groups meet together, view television clips, film clips, trailers, and whole films in conjunction with printed literature to uncover layers of meaning through observation, discussion, and re-viewing. → Scaffolds learning as students create a film trailer storyboard that argues for their reading of the text.	Create classroom activities in which students view, listen to, discuss, compose, and move to determine and analyze the central idea or theme of a wide variety of texts, presented in diverse media formats.	→ Uses printed text, a read-aloud, and blackout poetry to highlight a theme in *Macbeth*. → Crafts a unique viewing experience that includes multiple versions of the scene and setting, including images and sounds. → Uses goggles and physical experience to help students analyze and evaluate the theme of perspective in the play.
How Sarah's students enact the practice ↓	← Learning Practice →	How Steve's students enact the practice ↓
→ Analyze television clips, film clips, film trailers, and whole films in the context of literary selections, noting layers of meaning. → Discuss and analyze aspects of the film, central ideas, and themes with group members, refining and complicating their own ideas. → Compose a film trailer that represents their interpretation of the film. → Use both a personal reading of a film combined with close analysis to create storyboards for an original film trailer.	Read, view, listen to, discuss, experience, compose, and move to interpret, evaluate, and understand a wide variety of texts.	→ Receive and interpret information from the printed scene, an oral reading, the video footage of the scene performed, the storm experience, and the physical experience of using the goggles. → Compose an original blackout poem that highlights a "fair" or a "foul" reading of the scene. → Connect the theme of perspective through several diverse activities. → Apply and integrate this information to form an evaluation of the whole scene and play.

NCTE Principles Regarding 21st Century Literacies
Students create, critique, analyze, and evaluate multimedia texts.

See pages 130–131 for more on NCTE principles regarding 21st century literacies.

Common Core Anchor Reading Standards that intersect with these practices (CCSS, p. 35)

Craft and Structure
5. Analyze the structure of texts, including how specific sentences, paragraphs, and larger portions of the text (e.g., a section, chapter, scene, or stanza) relate to each other and the whole.

How Sarah enacts the practice	←——— Teaching Practice ———→	How Steve enacts the practice
→ Scaffolds students through process of close observation for cinematic, theatrical, and literary components of film. → Uses formative feedback to help students focus on power of chosen words and techniques to convey message in film trailer.	Encourage students to make connections between words, sentences, images, sounds, and spoken words in written, visual, and multimodal texts.	→ Focuses on specific words and lines of text that emphasize a theme. → Enables students to read, view, and listen to the scene multiple times in diverse formats. → Relates the central theme of the scene to other parts and scenes in the play.
How Sarah's students enact the practice	←——— Learning Practice ———→	**How Steve's students enact the practice**
→ Observe, discuss, and analyze smaller parts of the film and relate these parts to a reading of the whole film. → Deliberately use a text structure with attention to language and film technique to argue a particular reading of the film through the trailer genre.	Make connections between words, sentences, scenes, sounds, and images in written, visual, and multimodal texts.	→ Observe, discuss, and analyze specific word choices, lines of text, and whole scenes, relating these parts to a reading of the whole play through class discussion and writing.

NCTE Principles Regarding 21st Century Literacies
Students manage, analyze, and synthesize multiple streams of simultaneously presented information.

See pages 130–131 for more on NCTE principles regarding 21st century literacies.

Frames That Build: Exercises to Interpret the CCSS

The following are exercises that may be used by either individuals or teams of teachers to help determine how the standards intersect with classroom decisions.

- *Reading the standards.* Standards for visual literacy (for which NCTE has long advocated) are largely sporadic and appear as part of another strand in the CCSS (i.e., reading, speaking, and listening). Starting with the CCSS for reading, look for the language of thinking that can be taught through film. Further, anytime the words *perspective, bias,* or *argument* appear, consider how visual media become vehicles for constructing meaning around such concepts.

- *Weighing classroom decisions.* One facet of working with the CCSS to guard against is the creation of discrete assignments, each which may address components of the standards, but remain isolated from each other. To focus on the thinking and literacy skills that sustain authentic learning, collect a small sampling of assignments (three or four) that address reading, writing, speaking, viewing, and language. Determine what students are to learn in these, focusing on the skills you want to see them exhibit. When the focus is on the skills, where can the assignments converge into an experience? How might visual literacy be a vehicle for this learning? What concepts, instead of topics, can guide unit and lesson design?

4 Integrating Active Listening and Speaking Strategies

Teaching and Learning Practices for Speaking: Sarah's Classroom

Over the last couple of years I have been focusing on deliberately finding ways to craft the kinds of learning experiences for students that offer them value beyond school suggested by Newmann, King, and Carmichael (2007). In recent years my intentionality toward this particular facet of the learning process has been piqued and it's with this interest and focus that I set about crafting this unit for a junior/senior elective course, Heroic Men and Women. We spend a semester focusing on many traditional Greek mythological heroes, but I also want students to synthesize their work from throughout the semester and to situate that learning into a context of their own making. Thus, my colleague Rachel Mullen and I collaborated to construct a learning experience that would replace the traditional final and give students the opportunity to see their work throughout the semester collapse into this experience. Several weeks before the semester's end, I came to class with selected film clips and AFI's (American Film Institute) list of 100 Greatest Heroes and Villains. Using such divergent heroes as Atticus Finch, Indiana Jones, or George Bailey, students construct a definition of hero. Corresponding to that definition they analyze its antithesis through defining a villain using such examples as Norman Bates, Darth Vader, or the Wicked Witch of the West. Students use these definitions as a litmus for literary analysis as we carefully view M. Night Shyamalan's *Unbreakable*, an examination of the inextricable bond

> **Integrated Teaching and Learning**
>
> Here, Sarah asks students to employ critical viewing practices far beyond simply "watching a movie." Learners practice the skills of observation, finding patterns, and drawing conclusions about those patterns with film, just as they work on those skills when maneuvering any kind of critical text.

> **Collaboration**
>
> The use of these small, student-directed groups allows students to construct learning at their pace, use many of their own selected materials, and pursue their questions and interests. Students realize that their conclusions don't have to match their neighbor's, but that meaningful group work leads to heightened individual meanings.

between good and evil. Students employ their visual literacy skills as they look for camera angles, lighting, or editing that creates meaning; as they watch for transitions that signal shifts in tone or mood; as they listen to dialogue that reveals layers of character contemplation; and as they consider such topics as desire for power or the connection to Joseph Campbell's hero cycle.

Careful observation notes by the viewers coupled with a combination of small-group and whole-class discussion prepares students to continue to establish and construct their modern understanding of hero throughout a week of small-group-directed inquiry into a variety of texts. While not all student groups work with the same text at the same time, by the end of the week each student has (1) read and **analyzed** *Ultimate Spiderman: Power and Responsibility*; (2) **adapted** a modern-day interpretation of superhero into their own annotated sketch on reading selections from Owen King's *Who Can Save Us Now? Brand New Superheroes and Their Amazing (Short) Stories*; and (3) **compared** real-life heroes by reading an article about the Iditarod; reading an interview with Bob Kane, creator of Batman; and viewing selected interviews with comic book creators found on the *Unbreakable* Special Features portion of the DVD.

With a collection of texts, voices, and practiced skills, students culminate their reading, thinking, and discussion into an essay that uses evidence from the various texts to formulate a response to the prompt: How does the concept of hero and villain shape our world? Although this essay hearkens to a more traditional demonstration of learning, its placement in the unit allows it to be far more formative than evaluative. Students realize that the ideas they've crystallized in this work become the critical underpinnings of their upcoming project. This writing signals a shift in the unit wherein students transition from synthesizing the work of others to using their synthesis to devise thoughtful creations of their own. The final work of this unit emerges in three carefully scaffolded movements.

First, given our most recent work, coupled with the traditional Greek heroes we had spent the majority of the semester examining, I invite students to create their own original superhero, taking careful inspiration from individual proclivities coupled with those heroes and antiheroes we'd met throughout the course. Knowing that surmising the details of this character remains crucial to further success in the experience, I contemplated various templates that would elicit the right kinds of details. Inspiration came in the form of Facebook. Using a template, students create mock Facebook pages, complete with all kinds of details about their character manifested in the Facebook genre itself: the hero's friends, favorite quotes or music, recent wall posts, likes, and profile descriptions.

Integrated Teaching and Learning
Sarah's students read a variety of fiction, nonfiction, and informational texts under the auspice of exploring the concept of hero, which invites the texts to "talk to each other" rather than keeping them in isolation. Then, through the writing process, students are given feedback on their syntheses, language, and thinking.

Common Core State Standards
This kind of writing is evidence of students becoming independent learners, one of the themes that runs throughout the CCSS document.

Integrated Teaching and Learning
Using a contemporary application such as Facebook offers a way to embed the necessary thinking process in a genre that students recognize. Because students already understand this genre, they are able to focus on the work of creating a multidimensional character. Further, this work leads to a discussion about constructed realities and how they permeate twenty-first-century life.

Using either their own artistic talents or a website called *The Hero Factory*, students bring their character to life.

On creating the foundation for their final work, students demonstrate their persuasive writing skills (a skill central to the course) by nominating their hero for "Hero of the Year." Students submit an application by completing the nomination form and succinctly, persuasively answering such questions as (1) What single deed most defines this hero and *how* does this reveal his or her strong candidacy? (2) How do the values represented by this hero represent the way *you* see the world? (3) In recent years, honorees have included Luke Skywalker, Odysseus, Hector, and Achilles. Choosing one or two of these heroes, explain how the qualities of your nominee match or exceed the heroic qualities of our past recipients. As students manage these questions, they must situate their superheroes amid the work of the course, intertwining ideas, characters, and concepts.

The final phase of this experience provides yet one more sphere in which students are challenged to contextualize their heroes. Once nominations are drafted, finalized,

> **Integrated Teaching and Learning**
>
> Feedback and recursive process generate the kind of ownership that culminates as students progress through the project. Students realize that all kinds of communication—conferencing, practicing, conversation—enhance the thinking that will surface as they deliver their acceptance speeches.

and submitted, students prepare to deliver their acceptance speech as the Hero of the Year. They draft, discuss, get peer and teacher feedback, practice and revise, all in an effort to gain precision in their ideas and confidence in their public speaking. Then, instead of meeting in our classroom with straightened rows and sharpened pencils, the class meets in the auditorium where I have downloaded "hero music" onto my iPod and found some old trophies for the student-heroes to accept. As each student-hero comes to accept the Hero of the Year award and then delivers an acceptance speech *in* character, he or she situates the hero's work in light of a current political, social, or cultural issue. Therefore, the students must contextualize the hero's work in a way that gives the experience value beyond our school walls. By the time students conclude this experience and are ready to compose reflections on their learning, they realize how they progressed from someone else's list of what defines a hero, to constructing their own potential representative on just such a list. Offering students the environment in which to germinate their own learning reveals the infusion of their own questions and motivations with a close attention to the texts that influence such curiosities.

Sarah's Journey: Pathways to Enact These Practices

I didn't know I would be teaching this superhero unit when I started the work of piloting a new course called Heroic Men and Women, which was still clinging to a great deal of content from its predecessor course, Myths and Legends. As I anticipated teaching the course, I thought about how I crave mythology, how I love epics, and how I am fascinated by the allegory of it all. So when I started teaching this course for the first time, I imagined my students who signed up for the class would be just as eager. Certainly, there were those students who had spent many late nights with a flashlight under their bedsheets poring over long stories with prolific names and saturated with detailed plotlines. Yet, there were more who just simply "signed up" for the course. Of these students, one in particular, Aaron, challenged me. Each day Aaron would ask *why* we had to read about things that weren't real. He lamented about characters that weren't real, situations that would never happen, people whom he would never meet. So, I created this unit for Aaron and for all the students like Aaron who shared their similar dissatisfaction. If I was to meet my students right where they were, I had to rethink the course and determine how to still meet the course and district objectives while making the necessary adjustments to motivate and honor my students, just as they were. I spent time looking at the CCSS that guided the course, then took note of any available texts for this class or from those allocated for, but not being used by, other courses. Finally, I committed to including a formal speaking opportunity in a way that would create value beyond school. If Aaron was resistant to fiction, then he was nearly defiant about assignments that seemed irrelevant, that appeared to do little more than serve to accumulate point totals. With these self-imposed constraints, I sought out my colleague, Rachel Mullen, and through our conversations, this unit emerged.

It started with the idea of having students create their own superheroes. From there, I knew my students needed to "do something" with the superheroes; just creating them might be fun but would result in impotent learning. I started to think about the spheres of learning from the semester that could intersect in this kind of work: the previous heroes, the concepts they promoted, and the various ways in which students could demonstrate their learning. Thus, the concept of the Hero of the Year, complete with nomination application and formal speech, surfaced.

Yet careful scaffolding would need to be a priority. While some classes of students might thrive with an entire project presented to them, I had quickly learned that this class was successful with small, manageable steps, carefully working toward constructing its own learning, bit by bit. I began looking for a place in which students could anchor their thinking—first, the AFI 100 Greatest Heroes and Villains list, then the film with literary analysis, and next the short stories and informational texts. At each step I was careful to give students structures to help them manage and hold their thinking. By the time I asked them to create their own superheroes, they each had a reservoir of knowledge from which to draw.

Common Core State Standards
The standards, along with their attention to textual complexity, are one of the factors that can help teachers select the texts students read.

Scaffolding would be important not only in the design of the unit but also in the execution of it. Students received peer and teacher feedback throughout the entire process. The feedback appeared at different stages in their processes, but it was always formative: guiding, nudging, nonthreatening. Certainly, many surprises emerged.

Aaron was only mildly resistant to the idea; imagining a superhero via Facebook was a greater challenge in character development than students expected; using the nomination form required students to be more precise with their word choice; and the formal speeches emerged as some of the most successful in my twelve years of teaching. In part, the formal speeches were successful because they became the pinnacle of intense and varied work that was driven by students throughout the entire unit. I also think that because students delivered their speeches "in character," they were liberated from some of the awkward peer pressure that self-assured students often feel when delivering a speech to their peers at the front of the classroom. It was as if by becoming the character they had permission to *be* that character in a way they were hesitant to be about themselves in other formal classroom speeches. By focusing on my students, having a deep content knowledge of the curriculum, and being able to understand the guiding standards both intricately and broadly, I welcomed the opportunity to see thinkers emerge where fact-finders left off. Perhaps most importantly, for students like Aaron, each step was purposeful in an authentic way. In using authentic genres to house the critical thinking, he recognized a relevance that reduced his resistance.

Throughout the CCSS, there is a heightened resolve to elicit work from students that makes effective argument, that wields effective logic, and that demonstrates the ability to convey complex ideas. This superhero vignette highlighted a unit wherein students used public speaking to culminate in an experience in which many facets of literacy converged. In the next vignette, researcher Crystal VanKooten shares how another teacher, Nikie Jenkinson, also focuses on oral communication to teach effective argumentation.

Meet Nikie Jenkinson, Twin Lakes High School

Nikie Jenkinson teaches English and speech at Twin Lakes High School in Monticello, Indiana, which is a small, rural town in northern Indiana. Twin Lakes has many students from farming families, but some of Nikie's students also are part of families who have settled in Monticello from Chicago or Indianapolis. These students come from diverse backgrounds but are mostly white, with Hispanic students representing the largest minority group. Twin Lakes is on a block schedule, and Nikie teaches three eighty-eight-minute classes per day. Throughout the year, she teaches a variety of courses: English 9 and English 11, along with several sections of elective speech. Nikie uses a teaching style that she describes as cooperative and constructive, encouraging students to interact, take part in an activity, and cooperatively establish meaning from the materials provided.

Teaching and Learning Practices for Speaking in Nikie's Classroom

Many of the students at Twin Lakes take Nikie's speech class to recover a lost English credit or to graduate midterm, while others take it to better their chances at college admission and success. Whatever their reason for enrolling, in Nikie's class students find a place where they observe, analyze, and practice both verbal and nonverbal communication techniques that are grounded in NCTE principles and the CCSS. Together, Nikie and her students study how argument can occur through language and words, but also through voice, gesture, movement, and circumstance. These kinds of verbal and nonverbal rhetorical techniques are at the center of Nikie's lesson that uses analysis of either Obama's acceptance speech at Hyde Park or his 2009 student address as a springboard for students to compose their own persuasive speeches. This lesson enables students to identify, analyze, discuss, and then put into practice oral techniques for verbal and nonverbal communication, argument, and establishing credibility through activities such as viewing, class discussion and debate, partner work, and individual tutoring that center as much as possible on students instead of the teacher.

Nikie begins the lesson by writing a core set of objectives drawn from the CCSS on the board for students to see. After the objectives have been established orally, Nikie distributes a viewing grid to the students, which helps them apply their knowledge of rhetorical devices and communication strategies to evaluate a speech given by a public figure. This viewing grid (see Figure 4.1) asks students to pay attention to the various verbal and nonverbal persuasive techniques used by Obama in his speech that convey him as credible or questionable. The grid requires students to take

Common Core State Standards
One approach is to explicitly examine and talk with students about the language found in the standards themselves.

notes on verbal and nonverbal aspects of the speech that students find credible or questionable and record specific details from the speech that back up these assertions.

As the students watch the video recording of Obama's speech, they take notes on their grid about the rhetorical devices they observe. After viewing, the class discusses together the persuasive and rhetorical techniques that students noticed in the speech that made the speaker seem credible or questionable. A few students comment on the credibility of Obama's topic, word choice, and delivery in the student address: "He used current problems like using the Xbox too much or sitting in front of the TV too much. . . . He used current stuff." Another states, "He used casual vocabulary. He didn't weigh it down with really big words. He's talking to kids, so he wanted to be

Prepared Remarks of President Barack Obama Back to School Event: Arlington, Virginia; September 8, 2009			
	Circumstances: location, audience, external environment, media, viewing conditions	**Verbal Cues:** vocabulary, sentence structure, examples, statements, voice quality, pauses	**Non Verbal Cues:** gestures, facial expressions, interaction, eye contact, stance, posture
Credible: What does the speaker say or do that makes the audience believe him or agree with him?			
Questionable: What does the speaker say or do that calls into question his message, his motives, or his sincerity?			

Subject: Purpose:

Occasion: Speaker:

Audience: Tone:

FIGURE 4.1: A viewing grid.

understandable. He also changed his tempo a lot." Through listening and responding to comments like these, students work toward their own analysis of the speech and add to the information on their viewing grids. Students also comment on the aspects of the speech that made the speaker less credible. One student argues, "He talked about how we might not be president and we're not going to be professional basketball players. Aren't there kids watching this? Kids still might have hopes and dreams. It's way too harsh." Nikie listens to the students and often verbally prompts them to add to or refine their responses or invites others to respond as well.

Throughout this discussion, Nikie encourages her students to feel free to talk about a range of interpretations of the speech. Students in another section debate the purpose of Obama's acceptance speech at Hyde Park, some claiming that his speech was too personal and general and should have outlined a plan for the country in the next four years. Others in the class disagree, talking about the informality of the speech and citing evidence that Obama was surrounded by his supporters in his hometown and was responding to a special, hopeful occasion. Nikie uses debates like this to help students understand that speeches are developed for particular purposes and audiences, and that a speech's persuasiveness is contingent on multiple factors.

She encourages students to use specific evidence in their comments, and students follow Nikie's model, prompting one another to use specific evidence from the speech to support their statements.

After the discussion comes to a close, Nikie gives the students class time to plan and outline extemporaneous speech responses in which they must evaluate and support a position about Obama's speech using facts and specifics from the speech to back up the claim. During this time, Nikie offers one-on-one help to students throughout the class as they plan their speeches and draft outlines. Additionally, many students work together in pairs or groups, modeling for, instructing, and coaching one another in the production of their own pieces. Moving about the room, Nikie interacts with her students in a variety of ways, including monitoring off-task behavior, responding to frustration, answering student calls for help, and asking students about their progress as they plan.

To close the lesson, students present their extemporaneous speeches to the class. Students support their claims by using specifics from Obama's speech, including many points that were brought up in whole-class discussion. One student argues that Obama is credible due to his honesty, citing the way he bluntly told the schoolchildren that not everyone would be a professional basketball player. Another student argues that Obama's audience was able to relate to him, pointing to the way he presented his own past to the audience, stating, "How often do we have a president that can say 'I've been in your shoes?'" Many students use specifics like these to support their claim for their classmates.

Nikie's Journey: Pathways to Enact These Practices

As Nikie reflects on planning this lesson, she mentions that she started by having her own objectives in mind. She went in with the goal that students would be able to identify verbal and nonverbal messages and credible and questionable rhetoric in use. She also wanted students to be able to establish a claim about a speaker and a topic and support that claim with details from a source. She continued planning from these objectives, trying to imagine the best way to have students working and actively engaged through most of the lesson. Toward this end, Nikie favored viewing, partner work, and individual tutoring in the lesson instead of lecturing. While Obama's acceptance speech and the student address are not the only examples of oral rhetoric that incorporates verbal and nonverbal communication techniques, viewing, analyzing, and responding to these speeches gives students the cultural experience of viewing a political speech that many do not experience in their homes. They also have the power to analyze the words and actions of an important

 **Collaboration**

Sharing ideas and getting feedback are key elements in students' composing processes. This in-class work time is one place where students can have the opportunity to formulate and test their ideas, receiving feedback as they go. Students work individually and work together. Sometimes, Nikie offers advice and assistance to students, and other times, she steps back and encourages students to help one another.

 Honoring Diversity

A lesson like this could conclude in multiple ways. As time allows and after analyzing several of President Obama's speeches, for example, students could assume the role of one of his speech writers who must craft a response to a timely issue. This new speech could incorporate and contextualize effective rhetorical techniques elicited from analyzing multiple speeches.

speaker, which, as Nikie notes, gives them a feeling of credibility and responsibility in their work.

Many of the aspects of this lesson also build on students' prior knowledge. Nikie uses the brief oral introduction to remind students of concepts (such as analyzing an audience and context) and vocabulary (such as verbal and nonverbal cueing) that they already have and will need for this lesson, and the listening grid lists specific areas for student attention that help them remember lessons from past classes. During one-on-one interactions with students as they plan their speech response, Nikie pushes students to deepen their understandings of verbal and nonverbal communication techniques, asking them to consider their word choices and support more deeply.

As Nikie knows, a good lesson often does not work perfectly the first time but evolves over time through constant revision. Nikie describes how she rarely uses a lesson twice in the exact same format, stating, "I compare my lessons from one year to the next and cross-reference them with standards. If I use a lesson from the previous year, I revise it and try to make it more authentic to student interests." This approach allows Nikie to tailor her lessons first to student needs and yet still incorporate an attention to standards as she makes revisions to lessons from year to year. Nikie experienced how this lesson revision process can improve instruction as she taught, analyzed, and refined the lesson above, bringing it to its current form.

Nikie describes how in early iterations of this lesson, students focused more on creating an analogy as an opening attention grabber for their speech and less on evaluating and using verbal and nonverbal rhetorical techniques. She states, "The first time I taught this lesson, students became so hung up on creating an analogy for an attention getter at the beginning of their response that the attention getter detracted from my objectives. In later lessons, I asked students to create an interesting grabber to gain the audience's attention at the beginning of the speech. The analogy was only a suggestion, and students were able to focus more on the main lesson objectives." This narrative suggests that keeping clear objectives at the center of a lesson and crafting prompts and directions that do so, as well, can help to keep students on task and working toward the key learning objectives for which the lesson is designed. Many times, students aren't able to effectively process too many expectations at once, so beginning with a narrow focus on key objectives is wise, and more expectations, such as the use of analogy for an attention-getter, can be layered on later if necessary.

While Nikie begins planning a lesson like this one with her own objectives for her students in mind, standards also play a key role in the decisions she makes while planning. She describes a shift in her own thinking about standards from the beginning of her career to today: "When I first began teaching, I focused strongly on the state standards

Integrated Teaching and Learning

Nikie's Obama analysis lesson or Sarah's hero unit highlight ways that students can meet specific speaking standards, but as Nikie mentions, reading, writing, speaking, listening, language, and viewing often overlap and intertwine within lessons. Nikie's students read Obama's speech critically, write responses in various ways, listen and speak to one another, and in the end present their claims through spoken language.

and their multiple indicators for mastery. I found myself teaching many stand-alone lessons for the sake of covering a standard. The Common Core State Standards have influenced me to maintain a high quality of educational opportunity in the classroom in a more authentic way. I know that by focusing on multiple literacy strands and technology use in my lessons, I will be addressing true, rich standards in my classroom." Nikie's new approach to using standards does not involve teaching what she labels "stand-alone lessons" focused on a particular standard, but seeks instead to incorporate multiple literacy strands into lessons like this one that coincide with standards in an authentic way.

Nikie also describes how her teaching has become more responsive to student needs as she gains more experience in the classroom. She states, "Over the years, my teaching has become more flexible and organic as a response to students' needs as individuals, rather than rigid standards. I have gained confidence in knowing that by offering rich, standards-based educational opportunities in a cooperative, comfortable environment, I can help more students to improve their personal best skills." Thus, instead of focusing first on rigid standards, Nikie chooses to place and keep individual student needs at the center of her instruction, while still teaching for standards in embedded, authentic ways throughout the process.

Common Core State Standards

Like Steve Bodnar, Nikie approaches planning with the CCSS by keeping student needs at the center of her instruction first. For Nikie, specific attention to the standards themselves follows the consideration of these needs.

Nikie keeps student needs at the center of instruction by allowing students to voice their opinions and preferences, taking suggestions from students, modifying assignments if they still meet the same objectives, making diverse texts available for reference, and encouraging students to work within their area of interest. She tries to craft projects that are important to students, such as oration about a human interest or concern. For such a project, one pregnant teen in Nikie's class wrote about child abduction, while another girl, suffering from anxiety attacks, outlined her illness in objective terms. A different boy who lost his friend to a drug overdose spoke about teen suicide, while another wrote about the benefits of lowering the legal drinking age in Indiana. "These types of speeches," Nikie states, "often do lead to classroom debate at their conclusion, and keeping a cooperative, constructive tone in the classroom is one of my primary roles as the students express their opinions. The classroom emphasis on social behavior and interpersonal communication fosters student involvement and buy-in. Everyone has a voice."

Honoring Diversity

Just as Sarah reminds us of the importance of crafting learning experiences that have value for students outside of school, Nikie strives to build the kinds of assignments in her speech class that let students explore their own unique areas of interest.

Finally, Nikie has also evolved her approach to assessment over her career. Currently, she places more emphasis on lower-stakes, formative assessments that occur at multiple points throughout a lesson or unit instead of one high-stakes assessment at the end. Nikie begins to assess as she listens to and interacts with her students in class discussion, and follows up with this assessment when she works with individual students one-on-one as they plan their speeches. She is able to observe and push each student's understanding of verbal and nonverbal rhetoric as she meets with them. At the end of the lesson, Nikie uses the speech itself as another piece of the assessment. She states, "I have begun to use more projects and performances as assessments than I did in my earlier years. I no longer have the same compulsion to give a major exam to culminate a unit or grading term. Instead, I use quizzes and tests along the way. These formative assessments produce less anxiety in my students and myself. If the assessment does not go well, I can always refine instruction and give a new test . . . now, I realize that the experience in the classroom is so much more vital than the number in the grade book, and I focus on trying to make that experience as educational as possible." This approach to assessment keeps the student at the center of instruction, as lessons can be adapted and refined throughout a unit to better serve the students and help them to master the lesson objectives and related standards.

Charting the Practices

Even as reading, writing, speaking, viewing, and language are intertwined in our teaching, both lessons are also examples of students participating in tasks that align with the Common Core Speaking Standards. Our students frequently participate in formal speaking events at the conclusion of a learning experience. Yet, as the CCSS note, speaking is not just about giving formal speeches, it is also about managing communicative process and using interpersonal skills. The following charts highlight the NCTE principles and teaching practices embedded in our teaching, connecting these to specific Speaking Standards in the CCSS document. The chart also includes student learning practices and summarizes the tangible ways in which our students enacted these practices in the classroom.

Common Core Anchor Speaking and Listening Standards that intersect with these practices (CCSS, p. 48)		
Comprehension and Collaboration 1. Prepare for and participate effectively in a range of conversations and collaborations with diverse partners, building on others' ideas and expressing their own clearly and persuasively.		
How Sarah enacts the practice ↓	← **Teaching Practice** →	↓ **How Nikie enacts the practice**
→ Facilitates small-group and whole-class discussion of film clips, short stories, interviews, and articles. → Uses small-group-directed inquiry, which leads to the development of an essay and the final hero project.	Open a space for students to participate in a range of conversations and collaborations, while providing ongoing oral and written formative feedback to help students develop ideas and construct learning.	→ Uses whole-class discussion of Obama's speech. → Interacts one-on-one with students as they plan their speeches and allows students to interact with one another. → Encourages pop-up debates where students discuss and reflect over speeches.
↓ **How Sarah's students enact the practice**	← **Learning Practice** →	**How Nikie's students enact the practice** ↓
→ Discuss ideas and responses with classmates in whole-class and small-group setting. → Listen and respond to classmates' ideas. → Listen and respond to teacher feedback. → Refine and complicate their own ideas and interpretations.	Interact and share ideas with a partner, with a small group, with the whole class, and with the instructor. Listen to others' ideas and build understandings that take these into account.	→ Discuss ideas and responses with classmates in a whole-class setting. → Listen and respond to classmates' ideas. → Listen and respond to teacher feedback. → Refine and complicate their own ideas and interpretations.
NCTE Principles Regarding Speaking and Listening Expand participation in discussions; connect speaking and listening; foster active listening. *See pages 124–125 for more on NCTE principles regarding speaking and listening.*		

Common Core Anchor Speaking and Listening Standards that intersect with these practices (CCSS, p. 48)

Presentation of Knowledge and Ideas
4. Present information, findings, and supporting evidence such that listeners can follow the line of reasoning and the organization, development, and style are appropriate to task, purpose, and audience.

How Sarah enacts the practice	←——— Teaching Practice ———→	How Nikie enacts the practice
→ Asks students to read, listen, and view, gleaning information and supporting evidence. → Crafts the hero acceptance speech, given in character, in which students make a claim about the hero, situating the hero's work in light of a political, social, or cultural issue.	Create an authentic activity in which students gather information and evidence and then orally present a complex claim to an audience.	→ Asks students to listen and view, gleaning information and supporting evidence. → Crafts an extemporaneous persuasive speech, in which students must make a claim about Obama's speech and provide evidence for that claim.
How Sarah's students enact the practice	←——— Learning Practice ———→	**How Nikie's students enact the practice**
→ Craft and deliver hero acceptance speech in character to their peers, making a claim about the hero that is backed up with evidence and links the hero's work to a current political, social, or cultural issue.	Plan and execute an oral presentation in which a complex claim is presented to an audience. Reflect on the effectiveness of the presentation.	→ Craft and deliver extemporaneous persuasive speech to their peers, making a claim about the effectiveness of Obama's speech and providing specific evidence for that claim.

NCTE Principles Regarding Speaking and Listening
Support the development of formal speaking.

See pages 124–125 for more on NCTE principles regarding speaking and listening.

Frames That Build: Exercises to Interpret the CCSS

The following are some exercises that may help you to individually or as a team work to interpret the CCSS in a way that makes sense for your teaching context.

- *Reading the standards.* Looking at the language of the CCSS, consider the dynamic between teaching communication and teaching public speaking. Notice the places where both communication and public speaking emerge. As these places are targeted, look for the language of thinking and/or another skill that is shared in reading/writing standards.

- *Weighing classroom decisions.* Instead of imagining stacking communication assignments on top of reading assignments, on top of writing assignments, consider how these can be layered or how they can overlap. When does the communication work become the first draft of the paper? When does the digital media presentation (from speaking and listening) become the evidence of reading or research? Which kinds of authentic discourse situations would allow students to experience many strands of literacy?

5

Writing Is a Thinking Process Shared with Others

Teaching and Learning Practices for Writing: Sarah's Classroom

I recently stumbled on a few teachers who were discussing the notion of reteaching. One declared, "I never move on until I know students have got it right." Another honestly acknowledged how difficult that must be: "It's tough to keep everyone together. I'm not sure I can say every student masters a skill or concept before I move on to the next one." A third teacher added, "I give them everything they need to know before the test. If they don't pass, it's their responsibility." As the teachers dispersed, I contemplated what I had heard of the conversation, unsettled by its subtext: teaching is discerning between right and wrong; reteaching is navigating the difference between the two. Rather than seeing our engagement in the learning process as a series of "dead end" signs to be navigated with reteaching, there is incredible potential in being part of their process in a way that allows us to journey with them, nudging and suggesting, questioning and supporting, as they find their own way, linear or not.

This teachers' conversation mirrors the crux of what we know about literacy: it is recursive, complex, and most authentic when integrated. Certainly the process of each literacy strand (i.e., reading, writing, speaking, viewing, language) guides learners closer to autonomy; however, English teachers have the unique opportunity to synchronize writing process with formative assessment to energize student writing. Three of the CCSS found on pages 45 and 46 in writing call for students to write arguments that support claims using reasoning and evidence; to write narratives with well-chosen details; and to write explanatory texts that convey complex ideas and concepts. Each of these writing endeavors requires students to negotiate complex cognitive tasks and then make that complex work clear and convincing to the reader. To achieve this height of discourse, students will need to be engaged in a process that does far more than delineate between right or wrong, good or bad. They will need to be nurtured through a process that guides but resists managing student writers.

As I introduce more complexity to my students, I'm also building into their experience a greater attention to the process. Too often we can "get away" with not making our implicit learning process explicit when it comes to manageable tasks. Yet, as we work to challenge students with more complexity, we must simultaneously focus evermore on a nurturing process, equipped with scaffolding and recursivity. This reality is especially palpable in a unit, The Quest, which begins a senior-level course that asks students to consider a set of essential questions that serve to guide not just the unit, but the work of the year: (1) What drives humans to search for an ultimate truth? (2) Is the quest necessary for human survival? (3) How does the quest organize and guide a community of learners? On reading a collection of short texts—drama, short story, poetry, essay, and song—each addressing the idea of the quest or thinking from a different perspective, I give students their challenge: Devise your own system of thinking, using a metaphor or analogy to explain it. Whether it's likened to an inquiry-based exercise or a problem to solve, students must examine what it means to be a thinker. For example, Anna believes thinking occurs in stages, that you can't participate in the next stage until you've actualized the one you're in. Therefore, she uses the metaphor of a growing tree to illustrate her theory of thinking, being careful to note how external, environmental factors such as resources or experiences (like sun or water to the tree) affect the growth of the thinker. Differently, Josh believes that there isn't one kind of intelligence; rather, we all have strengths and it's our ability to capitalize on those strengths that determines one's success as a thinker. He chooses to use all the parts of a playground (a slide, a merry-go-round, a sandbox) to illustrate the implicit joy and significance of each distinct type of thinking. Not only are students challenged to be highly metacognitive about thinking, but then they have the added task of using a metaphor to explain these complex ideas. They may be explicating, but students quickly learn the tenuousness of making that complex idea in their brains clear to the reader.

A complex challenge like this requires scaffolding, which begins with a demonstration. Using an apple and an onion, I talk about two different kinds of thinking and how the characteristics of either type of produce represent a facet of thinking, for example, the idea that both an onion and thinking have layers or the notion that the "seeds of thinking" are protected by a core. Even though I begin this demonstration, we quickly begin working together as a class to complete various interpretations of apple and onion thinkers. Continuing the scaffolding process, students now work together in pairs or groups of three (of their own choosing) to devise and represent in posters their own *system* of thinking (which is generally more complex than an apple or onion representation of thinking). Working collaboratively fosters an environment that embraces a team approach to solving the problem of not only creating a system of thinking, but then determining an analogy or metaphor to illustrate that system.

Connections
Sarah plans her units around essential questions. For more information on using this approach in your planning, see page 97 in Section III.

Collaboration

Sarah asks her students to talk about their ideas for writing before committing them to paper. They rehearse their thinking, listen to others' ideas, and gather as well as offer feedback throughout the writing process that moves recursively between drafting and revising over time.

Common Core State Standards

By asking students to communicate their ideas to others and to offer feedback to others' ideas, Sarah's practice integrates Speaking and Listening standards into her writing lessons.

Once students complete their posters with illustrations, each group presents the idea to the class. Even this is an integral part of the process because students don't just stand in the front of the class, show their poster, wait for polite applause, and sit down. Rather, the audience is obligated to become involved. I explain that presentations are catalysts for conversations, so as audience members the students are responsible for asking questions that would require further thinking on the part of the presenters. This dialogue helps to inform the next step for students as they create their system of thinking, which may or may not draw on the work of the group. Individual students use journal writing to help devise their systems and then, as a whole class, we generate a substantial list of potential metaphors by focusing on "things that have parts." While the first round of brainstorming usually elicits a lot of everyday items such as a camera, car, or computer, later rounds include more complex offerings such as a playground, carnival, or rain forest. Helping students find the intersection between their ideas about a system of thinking, a parallel metaphor, and their own interests requires time and talk. They need time to try out different ideas and the opportunity to talk them through. Still, before drafting, students complete a series of part-to-whole analogies. This helps to slow down their thinking and offer them a foothold before embarking on the arduous task of clearly writing about such a complex process.

At the onset, our work in this unit may seem overly teacher-directed and may give the false impression that all students are undergoing a process to elicit a preconceived notion of how this writing will emerge. In reality, these are but a series of cognitive "warm-ups" designed to get students thinking in metaphor, talking in metaphor, and ready to focus on complex ideas. In other words, this is a problem to solve: their entrance into the problem requires cognitive leaps; likewise, their exit from the inquiry creates a commensurate complexity. As they draft, I anxiously anticipate the myriad ways in which students will approach their inquiry: one student submits a Socratic dialogue, another offers a fairy tale, some try to work within a conventional essay structure they've been raised on, while others vacillate between poetry and narrative. Creating the "reservoir" of knowledge may be teacher-directed, but how students find their way is decidedly determined by the writer.

At the end of the initial drafting process, each student is in a different stage of his or her writing. Some have it nearly hammered out, while others have found they don't know what they think about thinking. Yet other students have beautiful descriptions of their object, but haven't connected it to thinking. Still others have written a precise description of thinking, but the notion of metaphor has eluded them. As I respond to the drafts, I continue to resist the idea that it is right or wrong; rather, I recognize it as where they are in their process, for this piece of writing.

Throughout our course, our writing process takes on many different facets of garnering feedback. We involve peer feedback through online discussions and class interactions and we often have an audience that goes beyond our school walls. In this vignette, I've chosen to focus on the role of one facet of this process, teacher feedback. One of the most important "moves" of my teaching is to create a culture in which learners—writers—feel heard, safe, and able to take risks. At the early part of the year, when this particular unit occurs, I use my feedback to begin chipping away at the idea that they are writing a school assignment, that I am their audience. It's through the podcasts and subsequent conferences that I am able to *talk* with them about their work, not offer a set of corrections.

Having resisted the idea that a draft is right or wrong, I come to it without a rubric in hand or a set of preconceptions. I come to it as a fellow writer, as a fellow reader, as a fellow thinker. I would like to be able to carve out enough time in each class to conference with every student. Sometimes I can do that, but often our pacing is fast enough that I can't. When that happens, I create an individual podcast for each student. Beginning with a hard copy of the paper in front of me, as I read I use an "anchoring" number system. For example, if I want to start with the comment about the title, I'll write a "1" at the end and circle it. Functioning like handwritten footnote denotations, students may get comments on specific words, sentences, or whole paragraphs. Each anchor corresponds to spoken feedback that I create by generating a voice memo on my iPod. Students can expect to hear a variety of comments throughout the paper that range from technical advice on word choice or sentence composition to questions about how they came up with their ideas. To help students become more responsible for gauging their writing over time, at the end of each podcast I respond to the same six prompts, which are compiled into an acronym and corresponding action planning device: the GREASE monkey. By receiving extended comments from the same six categories—Grammar, Rhetorical strategies, Evolution of writing, Ask questions, Strengths, and Encouragement for revision—writers can track their feedback for patterns of growth or continued need. The acronym also reminds us that I'm just the mechanic, but they are in the driver's seat of their writing.

As a component of their revision, students listen to their podcast—which has been downloaded to iTunes, converted into an MP3, and emailed to students—and generate an action plan for revision based on the feedback and their own authorial choices. Once they receive their podcast, students have a week to revise, request further conferences, and

Honoring Diversity

Some teachers may not have access to the kind of technology Sarah talks about here. There are many alternate and inexpensive ways to offer feedback to students on their writing:
- Use tape recorders
- Comment in-text
- Log comments using online recording and storage sites
- Use free online shared collaborative document writing sites (such as a wiki or Google documents)

Integrated Teaching and Learning

Sarah incorporates a system to aid students in their acquisition of Standard Written English in her responses to drafts. She aims to work with students to help them identify and correct their own language mistakes. She lets a student know when he or she has, for example, a comma error in a line, and then it becomes the student's responsibility to find and manage missteps.

Integrated Teaching and Learning

Sarah explains why the student-generated action plan is so important: "It's crucial that students see themselves as authors who have the authority to make decisions about their writing. This action plan gives them the opportunity to take into consideration the feedback they've received, but to also articulate how they would like to begin their process of revision."

submit a final draft. In this sense, there isn't a single "due date" for all students; the timeline, as well as the feedback and process, is completely individualized for each writer.

Even though students have been receiving feedback since I first demonstrated the difference between apple and onion thinkers, I don't assign a letter grade to any of the work until the final draft. Taking grades out of the equation for as long as possible creates an important shift in the culture of our classroom: we don't talk about grades, we talk about learning and cultivating writers, which means giving them the time, space, and nurturing to grow.

Sarah's Journey: Pathways to Enact These Practices

Writing is thinking. To this end, cultivating writers means cultivating thinkers. The design of this unit demonstrates the necessity of incorporating all strands of literacy to give students the best opportunity to write about complex topics. If students are to write with clarity about intricate topics, then they must be given the opportunity to generate a reservoir of thought, trials, and triumphs to draw on. In an effort to make the implicit explicit, I want to reveal the teaching moves of this unit. Although they appear as a chronological list, it's important to know that they *function* recursively; in other words, I spiral these, often out of order, depending on a student's process and where the student's work may take him or her. Additionally, these phases of process create the space, resources, and nurturing for a writer-centered environment.

Organize. Essential questions organize the unit; therefore, encourage students to use content to contribute to the purposeful attainment of concepts. Organizing units around essential questions also promotes reading as though the texts are in conversation with each other. When we "get texts to talk to each other," we resist compartmentalizing them and resist compartmentalizing our thinking about them.

Read. Long before students can conceive of their own systems of thinking, they need to fill that reservoir with voices and ideas of others who have also made this journey. By employing reading circles, students are exposed to a rich layering of texts aimed at unpacking this topic.

Scaffold. Begin with modeling the thinking (apples and onions). Sometimes I hear teachers who are concerned about "modeling the assignment," afraid that doing so will inhibit the creativity and individuality students would have otherwise brought to the work. A valid concern, indeed, yet if we model a process, a skill, the thinking, we are empowering students with the confidence to use a process to construct, not re-create, their learning. Each step scaffolds the process in a slightly different way: students collaboratively devise and illustrate a system of thinking; they present and garner thought-provoking questions from

Integrated Teaching and Learning
Sarah explains, "Certainly the process of each literacy strand (i.e., reading, writing, speaking, viewing, language) guides learners closer to autonomy; however, English teachers have the unique opportunity to synchronize writing process with formative assessment to energize student writing."

the class; individually they journal; together we brainstorm potential subjects for metaphor; and they complete analogy formulas. Each step provides students with the kind of feedback that supports their personal construction of learning. There may be redirection, but there isn't reteaching, because everyone's process is equally valid and equally "right."

Offer a problem to solve. Learners are motivated when they deem the task before them worthwhile. Offering students a problem (in this case, the challenge to create a system of thinking and explain that system through metaphor) in which they aren't searching for a right answer, but rather for a personal solution, obliges them to complex thinking, to rely on the reading, the discussion, the illustrating, the listening they've done throughout the unit. This kind of learning addresses what the CCSS describe as rigor.

Feedback. Working so hard to get students poised for this complex writing task would be short-sighted if not for the individual feedback students receive and use. I didn't always respond to papers this way. I remember the late nights of marking in the margins, of pointing out rights and wrongs. I remember being bleary-eyed when returning them the next day, but confident they would be eager to revise. The polite students put them in their folders. The more outright would toss them in the recycle bin and I would fetch the papers out, reminding students, "I spent at least fifteen minutes on each paper. Now, you should spend at least double that on revision." But because my comments were from the perspective of teacher to student, not writer to writer or thinker to thinker, they really *could* make the suggested revisions in fifteen minutes because I wasn't challenging them to *think* differently. When I changed my behavior, I also changed theirs. Now, students ask for follow-up conferences and more feedback on more drafts. They consult peers and find readers outside of our classroom community.

It might be easy to assume that talking about a paper saves a lot of time in responding. I haven't found that these podcasts save me any time at all. What I have found, though, is that I can say a great deal more in fifteen minutes than I can write. I have found that students will often share the feedback with their parents who will listen to it with them. I have found that when I am talking to my student, I resist only being the editor. There are other realities to making the podcasts part of the teaching practice. I don't do the podcast for every assignment; I do them for the major process pieces, which is usually three a semester. While I do some of the podcasting out of class, I also find ways to make use of class time. Sometimes I can carve out several days in a row for in-class writing conferences. In those cases, I record our conversation and then convert that into a sound file and send it to the student. This is equally as valuable. Often students will leave a writing conference with a short memory of our conversation. Recording it allows them to have access to our discussion *as* they are revising.

Sometimes incorporating scaffolding and formative feedback seems like a natural extension of the culture of the classroom. Other times it can seem daunting. Regardless of where a teacher may find himself or herself along this continuum, embracing one's own learning process means embracing a culture of mutual learning. So, remember, taking a step along *your* continuum is significant.

The next vignette, highlighting Oak Park teachers, is an eager companion to this one. As researcher Danielle Lillge will show, this team's desire to create a more authentic community of learners coalesced in devising student-driven writing and learning environments.

Teaching and Learning Practices for Writing in the Oak Park Team's Classrooms

Writing instruction for the Oak Park ELA team is integrated into all aspects of classroom work. Oak Park students write every day in their ELA classes because the team teachers believe writing offers students opportunities to develop ideas that they care about. Whether sharing with classmates or with other audiences, the Oak Park teachers are inviting their students to think about writing's myriad purposes. Using a Writer's/Reader's Notebook to log their thinking through writing, Oak Park High School students spend a lot of their time writing to make sense of their learning. They approximate and imitate writing models and evidence their thinking concretely using writing. Sometimes students' writing takes the form of a notebook entry related to a reading assignment. Other times students write in relation to a particular writing strategy minilesson. Students also write in their notebooks as bell work to collect their thoughts prior to discussion. While viewing a movie excerpt, students write to create theories and identify claims and evidence. Oak Park students revise notebook entries to explore which entries they'd like to develop further. No matter the particular writing approach, as the snapshots below describe, the Oak Park teachers employ instructional strategies that help students create and develop ideas in their writing.

Common Core State Standards

The teachers ask students to use the sticky notes to enact Reading Standards for Literature 3 and 5. Linda points out that the sticky work is "also limited by number to focus work and develop students' selective use."

Students in team members' classes use sticky notes to write almost every day about their reading. This writing asks students to record their thinking, but the writing process itself also serves to extend and complicate their thinking about the text. Students ask questions, make predictions, record reactions, and annotate the text with their thinking as they read. For Ann, this writing "shows that they're thinking; rather than zoning out." And as Peter describes, this process of "active reading" engages students in the thinking that empowers them to negotiate and make meaning of difficult texts with independence. But the sticky notes themselves are not an end point to writing about reading. In Peter's classroom students write about characterization in their notebooks using the evidence from their sticky notes. For the Oak Park team members and their students, the sticky note writing serves as a launching pad for further thinking and synthesizing in notebook writing to explore particular aspects of as well as synthesize thoughts about their reading.

Students also write in other ways. Ann pages through her students' notebooks where they record their ideas as she explains the various ways that students use their Reader's/Writer's Notebook: "We have writing about writing and writing about reading, and their notebooks facilitate this process." The notebooks where students log all of their work serve as a record for students of how their writing develops in different ways across the semester. But the notebooks also enable Ann to talk about how her instruction and assessment evolve over the course of the semester to expect different things of students' writing. Early in the semester Ann's unit on personal narrative writing served in part to orient students to an interactive workshop model where their ideas in writing were valued over perfection. She explains, "My focus [in the Writer's Notebook] wasn't on having a perfect paper; it was on getting [students to] get their thoughts down. When they type . . . they're so concerned about mechanics. I had kids when I was going around the class who were all tied up in how to spell this; I had to keep saying that it doesn't matter because you have to get your ideas down." Ann recognizes that her students' inordinate focus on mechanical correctness emerged at least in part from prior learning about what is valued in writing assessment. So she intentionally chose not to ask students to publish a piece for quite some time so that she could orient students to the interactive workshop where she wanted them first to develop ideas to share with others before considering mechanical or editing issues.

Common Core State Standards

The Oak Park teachers integrate Common Core Language Standards into their writing instruction. NCTE Principles recommend that students learn how language works to become effective writers, and this is best accomplished by instruction that focuses on a context-based approach. Students benefit most from exposure to language instruction within the context of writing assignments that invite them to understand how to make choices about language use that reflect the purpose and audience for their writing.

Using a series of minilessons to offer students different strategies for generating ideas and developing ideas for more than a week, Ann first models for students a particular strategy in her own notebook before asking them to try out that strategy. One minilesson, for instance, asks students to think about a time they experienced extreme emotion as one way of generating an idea for writing a personal narrative. After identifying this as the purpose of the lesson, Ann continues, "What I would do first is create a list of different times that I experienced extreme emotion." Ann models by thinking aloud about each idea that comes to her mind, why it comes to mind, and how the idea might be worth writing about as she records these ideas in her notebook. In a later conversation, Ann details why she chose to model this generative process before ever handing out an example of a completed text, even a notebook entry draft. She explains her rationale for this decision: "I don't always hand out something completed because I want to show [students] my thinking and that I too struggle with these things." For her students, this helps them see that she is "real" too. In fact, they are often surprised by what Ann is willing to share. But in return, students begin to open up and share their struggles and experiences.

After Ann models, she invites students to turn to one another to work in pairs or partners so "they can talk about" their ideas in relation to the minilesson and writing-specific strategy. Ann's rationale for this decision comes from an interest in helping students rehearse what they write before committing ideas to paper, so they "can understand" both more deeply before turning to independent writing on their own. Other times students write in their notebooks before turning and talking to gather audience feedback on their ideas. Ann leads students in seven or eight of these mini-lessons before they ever reach the point of identifying what to write about in a more formal piece. At this point students use sticky notes to mark up their own writing just as they do with the texts they read. They use the sticky notes to highlight questions for further inquiry in their writing revisions. Students in Ann's class therefore revise before and as they draft. The sticky notes encourage students to dialogue with their own ideas, extend them further, or take them in a different direction; beyond these important steps, the notes also serve to make public students' thinking about and decisions about their writing in an effort to help students and teachers see how their writing evolves through careful, skillful decision making.

At the point when students choose one idea they want to develop further into an extended piece, Ann asks students to place their ongoing work on a particular project in a project folder so they can, she describes, "see where they are" as well as how their writing develops. When students move on to another project, the portfolio folder houses all of the work from each unit, including their project folder and finished products. The portfolio folder contents enable students to see how their writing has evolved across the course at the end of the school year. Ann's students are able to assess their own progress as writers and thinkers. They are able to begin to see the work contained in their Project Folder as a launching pad for further writing and thinking that will propel their ideas forward toward greater complexity as they experiment with new genres and ideas.

The Oak Park Team's Journey: Pathways to Enact These Practices

The Oak Park ELA team's approach to writing instruction is inherently linked to all ELA threads in discourse-oriented, interactive classrooms and results directly from their collaborative study with one another. Instructional collaboration with colleagues is a relatively new facet of the Oak Park teachers' experience, which results from the newly formed department as well as their commitment to redefine the school culture. In years past, teachers were often expected to meet with outside experts hired to fix things. Teacher collaboration was not prized as a form of professional development that empowered teachers to take an active role in learning about the instructional approaches that would best support their students' learning.

With the support of Linda, the ELA team teachers are beginning to see the value of collaborative study in reshaping their instructional plans. In contrast to years past, the ELA team teachers are beginning with their own classroom inquiry and the CCSS to inform their decision making. The following elements of this collaborative study begin to explain why this approach is making a difference in the team's instructional changes aimed at improving students' learning and classroom interactions.

- *Self-study/Student-study*—Team teachers talk regularly about "becoming students of our students." Using action research, team members are increasingly using their own notebooks, or Research Journals, to log their learning and collect data about their students' progress. They are beginning to develop research questions to guide their inquiries. As Ann and Peter illustrate in earlier vignette snapshots in this chapter, the team teachers take opportunities during class to collect data—in short conferences and through observations as they move around the classroom—which inform their decision making about adjustments to classroom instruction and which they bring to the team for further discussion.

- *Common units*—Focusing first on the eleventh-grade classes, the Oak Park ELA team has chosen to enact common units of study. These units of study have developed around the CCSS and the discourse-oriented, interactive workshop approach. Using common units enables team teachers to focus on their instruction and to talk regularly about necessary adjustments in response to the data they are collecting. The common units afford the team the opportunity to focus discussions on shared instruction and student learning rather than on one another's individual practices, thus eliminating what might otherwise become a threatening conversation. And since they're all in this new inquiry and enactment together, they can come together on equal footing to share their experiences and questions.

- *Core readings*—Team members have agreed on texts for each unit that serve as fulcrum texts for modeling the reading and writing habits of mind, skills, and strategies that outline each unit's goals and objectives. The team finds that it's easier to study students across classes if they share texts; it's easier to come to the group with questions that others value because they are working with the same texts and potential dilemmas. As such, the focus of the team's discussions is not on content but

Connections
Team members' use of readings is grounded in the NCTE principle that writing and reading are related. For further details about this relationship, see the appendix of NCTE principles (Appendix B).

rather on how they are using the core texts in support of students' learning of habits, skills, and strategies that scaffold their learning toward greater self-sufficiency. That said, however, team teachers still leave room for individual decisions about supplementary texts, especially when the data they collect suggest that students need further instruction and intervention.

- *Common local, formative assessments and instructional artifacts*—Using shared locally developed formative assessments to gauge students' learning and make instructional adjustments as well as other instructional documents or artifacts also opens the space for dialogue about practice for ELA team members. Through shared units of study, the teachers are able to bring to the table common artifacts, such as student writing, to identify patterns that transcend classes. These patterns then allow teachers to make collective decisions about how to adjust, proceed, or plan ahead within and beyond the unit of the moment.

Common Core State Standards

The Oak Park teachers leverage the CCSS to define the goals and pace of instruction.

The unit plan as an artifact also facilitates teachers' interest in making sure they move instruction forward. With the omnipresent concern about students' ability to pass high-stakes exams, Oak Park teachers are increasingly aware of the need to make sure their instruction keeps pace with colleagues' instruction so that they can collectively address grade-level CCSS before the state exam in the spring. Since the team meets regularly to assess students' progress and make adjustments to the units, their interest in pacing comes from their collective local concerns in relation to the test.

Instructional artifacts and teachers' formative assessments also offer early data that students as well as teachers are seeing shifts in students' thinking and writing. Due to these data, the Oak Park teachers have realized the need to implement lessons that help students see, through teachers' explicit modeling as Ann's snapshot above illustrates, just how they can use and live in their Writer's Notebooks and what this approach offers them as writers. Ann notes how students' writing "is deeper than it used to be; it seems they pick up more" from their reading and from the minilessons using the interactive workshop approach.

The sustainability of the team's collaboration is not without struggle and uncertainty. The Oak Park ELA team teachers have taken huge leaps into the unknown by agreeing to adopt a discourse-oriented, interactive workshop approach and to work with colleagues in collaborative study. Team teachers share honestly their concerns about how to best involve the special education teachers in the instructional shifts and interactive classroom culture, how to address instructional variability within the department, how to invite new open-enrollment students into a classroom community (especially when teachers spent a semester establishing norms for supportive discussion), and how to build students' competence across grade levels through shared language and study. Whereas they might have at one time seen these as insurmountable obstacles, the collaborative study model has provided team teachers with language and an approach that gives them cause to see how these questions can become the heart of their collaborative inquiry. Like the elements of the discourse-oriented, interactive workshop they have all adopted, the team's commitment to ongoing, deep collaborative study serves as another key pillar of their instructional shifts. And their commitment to collaborative study remains motivated by the early progress they note in their students' learning as a result.

Charting the Practices

The following charts highlight some of the key pedagogical understandings about and teaching practices for writing instruction that I, and the Oak Park ELA team, work to enact. Connecting these to specific Writing Anchor Standards in the CCSS document and merging how teachers expect students to evidence their ability to enact the standards in their learning continues to demonstrate the potential triangulation of the CCSS, NCTE principles, and classroom teaching practice.

Common Core Anchor Writing Standards that intersect with these practices (CCSS, p. 41)

Production and Distribution of Writing
4. Produce clear and coherent writing in which the development, organization, and style are appropriate to task, purpose, and audience.
5. Develop and strengthen writing as needed by planning, revising, editing, rewriting, or trying a new approach.

How Sarah enacts the practice	← Teaching Practice →	How Oak Park teachers enact the practice
→ Using the apple/onion demonstration serves as a way for her to model thinking. → Generating podcast feedback models for students how readers respond to writers' ideas and thinking.	Model for students how writers think, work, and solicit and use feedback from others.	→ Using minilessons in the workshop framework including a portion of the lesson where teachers model what they will expect students to try in their writing or talking about writing.
How Sarah's students enact the practice	← **Learning Practice** →	**How Oak Park students enact the practice**
→ Drawing on the apple/onion demonstration to develop their own thinking model in collaboration with others. → Creating an original system of thinking and using the writing process to explain it using analogy.	Students enact the skill, strategy, or thinking they watched their teacher model with others and individually.	→ Discussing ideas and responses with classmates in a whole-class setting. → Listening and responding to classmates' ideas. → Listening and responding to teacher feedback. → Refining and complicating individual ideas and interpretations.

NCTE Principles Regarding Writing
Writing is a process.
Writing is a tool for thinking.
Everyone has the capacity to write, writing can be taught, and teachers can help students become better writers.

See pages 122–123 for more on NCTE principles regarding the teaching of writing.

Common Core Anchor Writing Standards that intersect with these practices (CCSS, p. 41)		
Production and Distribution of Writing 5. Develop and strengthen writing as needed by planning, revising, editing, rewriting, or trying a new approach. *Range of Writing* 10. Write routinely over extended time frames (time for research, reflection, and revision) and shorter time frames (a single sitting or a day or two) for a range of tasks, purposes, and audiences.		
How Sarah enacts the practice	◄── **Teaching Practice** ──►	**How Oak Park teachers enact the practice**
→ Using presentations as a way for students to gather feedback on their ideas for writing. → Building in time for students' varied processes for writing into her units. → Offering feedback using GREASE monkey remains consistent across assignments to offer students individualized feedback.	Use instructional tools and formative assessments to support all writers' strengths, needs, and processes.	→ Offering individualized feedback during regular conferences with students. → Using regular "Quick Sort" observational formative assessments to adjust instruction. → Collecting student writing artifacts to talk about how to adapt instruction.
How Sarah's students enact the practice	◄── **Learning Practice** ──►	**How Oak Park students enact the practice**
→ Listening and responding to classmates' ideas to help them expand and reshape ideas for writing. → Using feedback to revise their writing at different stages in their process.	Use feedback from their teachers, peers, and others to identify their strengths, needs, and processes for writing.	→ Talking with one another regularly to gather feedback to revise their ideas and writing. → Drawing on feedback from their teacher in conferences to revise their writing.

NCTE Principles Regarding Writing
Writing has a complex relationship to talk.
Literate practices are embedded in complicated social relationships.
Assessment of writing involves complex, informed, human judgment.

See pages 122–123 for more on NCTE principles regarding the teaching of writing.

Frames That Build: Exercises to Interpret the CCSS

The following exercises may be used by individuals or teams of teachers who are interested in working through the standards. As you unpack the standards, the vignettes may provide a lens through which to view your own individualized implementation of the standards.

- *Reading the standards.* Read through the writing and language standards for the 9–10 and 11–12 grade bands. As you read, look for what differentiates the grade bands. Also, look for the "thinking" language implicit in the standards. Which thinking skills will need to be taught to implement the standards?

- *Looking at exemplars.* Download Appendix C of the CCSS, Examples in Student Writing, and look at sample pieces of writing for the high school  grade bands. What seems to be valued in these samples? Triangulate an exemplar, with a classroom rubric and sample writing from your classroom. What does this comparison elicit? Does the language in your rubrics and the student samples make way for the kinds of thinking determined in exercise #1?

- *Weighing classroom decisions.* On determining what you most value in the teaching of writing (e.g., process, different genres, authentic audiences), consider how to maintain those priorities while taking the standards into consideration. Where can the language of the CCSS make it into rubrics and the feedback offered to students? What kinds of writing do we need to continue to make room for in instruction?

III

Building

⊚ Introduction

At this point, you may be thinking to yourself, *Where do I begin?* There are many concerns competing for your attention as a teacher. Many students with diverse needs pass through your classroom door on a daily basis, and you have developed outcomes, goals, and objectives to guide your instruction in meeting these students' needs. To this end, you have established practices and ways of assessing student learning in your classroom. You bring your professional pedagogical content knowledge to the classroom, providing expertise in reading, writing, speaking, and listening for students. You teach within a specific context as well, considering the needs of your community and the demographic populations that you serve. With so many issues pressing in on teachers from all directions, aligning and shifting your teaching practices with the CCSS may feel like one more task heaped onto your already full plate.

Getting started by pulling back to view the big picture may help to put things into perspective and make first steps seem less overwhelming. As Figure 6.2 (see p. 92) suggests, considering the CCSS as part of the deliberate teaching and learning choices you already make can continue to help you keep students at the center of instruction while planning, enacting teaching practices, and assessing student learning.

Just as most of us could not wake up one morning and decide to run a marathon on will alone without significant prior conditioning, so too it is important to remind yourself that planning, teaching, and assessing with the CCSS will not be instantaneous, but will become part of your ongoing work over time. In this section, we focus on building instruction *from* and *with* the CCSS. As noted in Section I, building with the CCSS in mind does not mean checking boxes for individual standards; it means integrating a careful examination of the CCSS with the contexts and practices of our classrooms, always putting students at the center. The chapters in this section offer three approaches to this process of building: individual, collaborator, and advocate.

- *Individual*—There *are* things that you individually can do to keep students at the center of your work. In this section we discuss how you can read the CCSS document to help you plan instruction with the CCSS.

- *Collaborator*—We invite you also to think about how to collaborate with colleagues in planning and assessing with the CCSS, especially within and across grade levels.

- *Advocate*—In this section, we explore how you can use your knowledge about the CCSS and their language, along with your collaborative efforts, to advocate for the professional supports that will help you advance your students' learning needs.

Rest assured that like marathon preparation, you cannot be expected to successfully tackle all three of these roles expertly as you begin your journey with the CCSS. Nor do we share these three roles to argue that you need to consider them sequentially or even fully. As you well know and as our experiences suggest, this process will be inherently like conditioning for a marathon. There will likely be great strides forward, plateaus, and at times struggles. But as the vignette teachers in this book illustrate, with the support of others near and far, holding the vision for what *can* be will sustain and affirm where you are headed.

6

Individual Considerations: Keeping Students at the Center

In reading this book, you have already begun considering how the CCSS pose new challenges that suggest you rethink and shift instruction. Reassure yourself that the CCSS do not have to call into question quality teaching practices, NCTE Principles, and research. But the CCSS may ask you to rethink the complexity of *what* you teach. The charts at the end of each vignette chapter are a beginning effort to illustrate *how* and *why* we can and should be concerned about helping students negotiate increasingly complex learning tasks and texts; additionally, this chapter will help further articulate *how* you can plan with this goal in mind.

Reading the CCSS Document

Collaboration

At the 6–12 level, the Literacy in History/Social Studies, Science, and Technical Subjects strands share the reading and writing Anchor Standards. The CCSS send a strong message that reading and writing as part of developing student literacy within discipline-specific classrooms is the responsibility of all teachers working together.

The first step will be for you to individually negotiate and understand how the organization of the CCSS document requires close attention to detail. As we mentioned in Section I, the CCSS are grouped first by strands: K–5 and 6–12. These strands share strand sets, or College and Career Readiness Anchor Standards, in reading, writing, speaking and listening, and language. There are ten reading, ten writing, six speaking and listening, and six language Anchor Standards in each strand. Each Anchor Standard is then further detailed in grade-specific standards. The Anchor Standard is the foundation of the grade-specific standards, but the grade-specific standards include more detailed language to further describe what the expectation is for students in each grade; therefore, there are some grade-specific standards that include sub-standards with numerals that further delineate such details. As Figure 6.1 illustrates, the grade-specific standards track for each grade level until ninth grade, when the standards are grouped in two sets: ninth and tenth grades in the first set, and eleventh and twelfth grades in the second. The CCSS document describes this decision as one

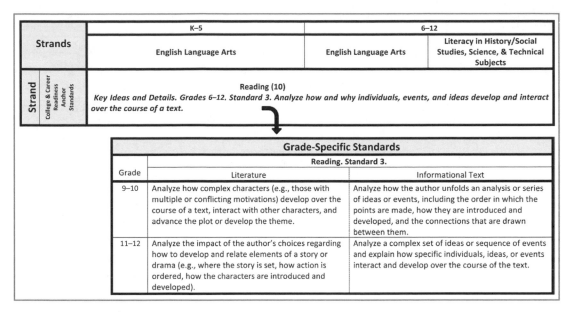

Strands	K–5	6–12	
	English Language Arts	English Language Arts	Literacy in History/Social Studies, Science, & Technical Subjects

Strand / College & Career Readiness Anchor Standards	Reading (10) *Key Ideas and Details. Grades 6–12. Standard 3. Analyze how and why individuals, events, and ideas develop and interact over the course of a text.*

Grade-Specific Standards		
	Reading. Standard 3.	
Grade	Literature	Informational Text
9–10	Analyze how complex characters (e.g., those with multiple or conflicting motivations) develop over the course of a text, interact with other characters, and advance the plot or develop the theme.	Analyze how the author unfolds an analysis or series of ideas or events, including the order in which the points are made, how they are introduced and developed, and the connections that are drawn between them.
11–12	Analyze the impact of the author's choices regarding how to develop and relate elements of a story or drama (e.g., where the story is set, how action is ordered, how the characters are introduced and developed).	Analyze a complex set of ideas or sequence of events and explain how specific individuals, ideas, or events interact and develop over the course of the text.

FIGURE 6.1: Reading the CCSS with an example.

that was meant to reflect the numerous elective courses at the high school level where there are fewer grade-level-specific courses. You will also notice that the CCSS focus a great deal on the kinds of reading students encounter across the school day, spelling out reading expectations for literature and informational texts. And at the K–5 level, the CCSS also include foundational skills standards.

An example of how this organization plays out in grades 9–10 may be helpful in explaining further. You'll note in Figure 6.1 an example of how you can read the CCSS for further specificity about grade-level distinctions using the first heading and Anchor Standard for reading. When you read the CCSS document, we encourage you to read for these distinctions between grade-specific standards. This will help you identify *what* students in the grade(s) you teach will be expected to enact or demonstrate proficiency doing.

Keeping Students at the Center

Reading the CCSS document with an eye toward distinguishing *what* students at the grade level(s) you teach will be expected to enact will help you keep your commitment to students at the center of your instructional decision making. Figure 6.2 illustrates how the multiple factors teachers consider when planning instruction speak to one another through teachers' knowledge of and interaction with students. As a teacher, all of your work with students happens in close relation to the context where you teach, including your school and local community. So your students' needs, abilities, and interests—both individually and collectively—inform your decisions about planning for, enacting, and assessing instruction.

Keeping students at the center will enable you to prioritize what to attend to first and why. Furthermore, keeping students at the center may also empower you to utilize the CCSS mandate to advocate for your students' unique learning needs, as we discuss later in Chapter 8. Our collective teaching experiences across the country suggest challenges are inherent to good teaching—whether a result of the CCSS or not, but foregrounding student learning needs, abilities, and interests provides a useful and necessary lens through which to interpret and implement the CCSS. No matter the pathway you choose, as Figure 6.2 illustrates, your students provide the map for planning and journeying with the CCSS.

Instruction that keeps students at the center often begins by asking what knowledge is available about the needs, abilities, and interests of student learners, and

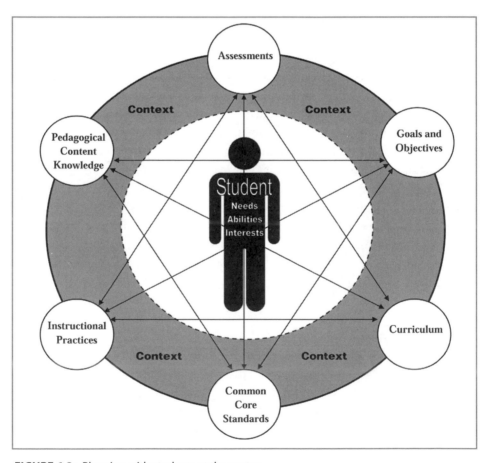

FIGURE 6.2: Planning with students at the center.

applying this knowledge to instructional decisions made about goals and objectives, curriculum, the CCSS, instructional practices, pedagogical content knowledge, and assessment. Figure 6.3 contains the types of questions you might ask yourself as you begin to consider the knowledge you have about students and how this can shape your instructional decisions in response to the CCSS. Answering the questions in Figure 6.3 also involves careful consideration of your teaching context in relation to what you know about your students by asking about the community, family and home cultures, out-of-school experiences, and school and district culture that influence your students' schooling experiences and your instructional decision making.

Figure 6.4 provides a list of these questions that you can use as a beginning point for instructional planning. Your answers to these questions will help you enact

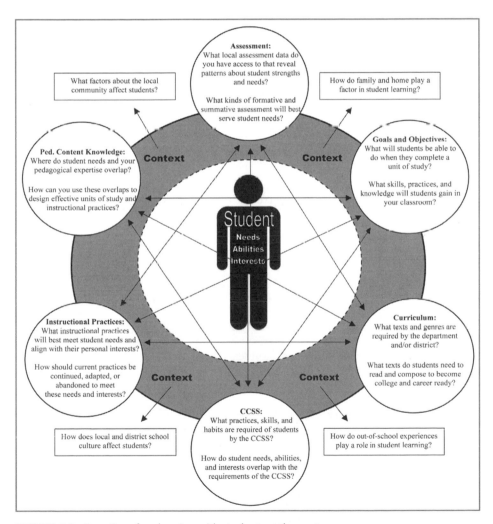

FIGURE 6.3: Questions for planning with students at the center.

What do I know about my **students** that supports my planning?

- Their needs –

- Their abilities –

- Their interests –

- Including:
    o Their home and heritage languages –

    o The funds of knowledge they bring from their homes and local communities –

    o The literacies students bring into the classroom –

Your Local Context

What factors about the local community affect students?

How do family and home play a factor in student learning?

How do out-of-school experiences play a role in student learning?

How does local and district school culture affect students?

FIGURE 6.4: Questions for planning template.

Assessment	Goals and Objectives
What local assessment data do you have access to that reveal patterns about student strengths and needs?	What will students be able to do when they complete a unit of study?
What kinds of formative and summative assessment will best serve student needs?	What skills, practices, and knowledge will students gain in your classroom?

Curriculum	CCSS
What texts and genres are required by the department and/or school district?	What practices, skills, and habits are required of students by the CCSS?
What texts do students need to read and compose to become college and career ready?	How do student needs, abilities, and interests overlap with the requirements of the CCSS?

Instructional Practices	Pedagogical Content Knowledge
What instructional practices will best meet student needs and align with their personal interests?	Where do student needs and your pedagogical expertise overlap?
How should current practices be continued, adapted, or abandoned to meet these needs and interests?	How can you use these overlaps to design effective units of study and instructional practices?

(Figure 6.4 continued)

teaching practices that support students' growing ability to make meaning of increasingly complex texts and enact increasingly complicated learning tasks. This approach, essential to CCSS, can be described as spiraling instruction, and it's the approach that the vignette teachers you've read about use; below we detail how this approach can help guide your individual planning for the students in your classroom.

Spiraling Instruction

As English language arts teachers, we know how difficult juggling the tasks of each day can be. Large class sizes, stacks of papers to grade, and limited collaborative and planning time often seem to get in the way of focusing fully on the needs of learners. At times, it may seem easier to plan lessons as lists of tasks just so you can make it smoothly through the day. In the past, we too have sometimes planned lessons in this way, using a monthly or a weekly calendar and filling the time with activities that aim in an unarticulated way at the objectives, skills, and practices we have in mind for students. Over time, however, we have come to view our planning differently, and this shift in our thinking and planning has actually increased the quality and complexity of the thinking and work of our students. In large part, this shift in our practice resulted from understanding how ELA instruction may differ from other content areas.

Unlike other content area instruction, which might be seen as building students' understandings and skills linearly, ELA learning can be seen as spiraling recursively. Research supports instructional planning that provides students with multiple opportunities to revisit concepts and enact their learning over time with increasing difficulty as more successful than planning and instruction that marches students through sets of activities and tasks. Planning this kind of instruction that spirals learning affords students opportunities to develop ELA understandings and skills within and across lessons, units of study, and courses.

As we've already discussed and as Figures 1.1 and 6.1 help to illustrate, the CCSS embed text complexity within the Anchor Standards. Thus, increasing the complexity of tasks and reading is one way to spiral your instruction. Additionally, the grade-level-specific standards grouped around the same Anchor Standards can prove helpful in that they point out specific skills and practices students can work on in a particular grade level and suggest the expectation that students will add to and refine these skills as they move from one grade to the next. Spiraling instruction within grade levels is often referred to as horizontal alignment whereas spiraling instruction across grade levels is often referred to as vertical alignment. The organization of the CCSS, as outlined in Figure 1.1, can help you consider how to plan and align ELA instruction horizontally and vertically. Below, we'll focus on how you can plan instruction that spirals in your own classroom, but in Chapter 7, we'll return to this idea of horizontal and vertical alignment through a discussion of collaboration.

Planning Units of Study

Identifying how to begin planning units of study that spiral ELA instruction and meet the CCSS demands can feel like a daunting task. But after identifying CCSS grade-specific expectations as well as your local approaches to asking students to demonstrate the learning and skills these expectations outline, you'll be ready to consider planning units.

Connections
"Units of study," in the chapters that follow, refers not to the teaching of specific texts but to designing groups of tasks, activities, and assessments that seek to meet an articulated set of goals, objectives, essential questions, themes, or genres.

Whether you are designing for the first time or revisiting previously taught units of study with your students' needs as the primary lens for shaping your instruction, there are multiple ways that you might choose to develop your units of study. The following list highlights some of the overarching approaches other ELA teachers have chosen to guide the development of their units of study:

- *Thematic*—around themes that ask students to grapple with shared human experiences (e.g., loss, love, courage, heroism, empathy)

- *Essential questions*—around questions worthy of students' attention without easy right or wrong answers that ask students to seek understanding to act with resolve; many of these questions illuminate what it means to be human, how humans choose to respond to pressing issues, and ask students to wrestle with uncertainty and complexity (e.g., Under what circumstances are people justified in questioning authority? What is the cost of progress? Why is literature worthy of study?)

- *Genre study*—around particular genres or multigenres that offer students opportunities to study literature within the genre as fulcrum texts for students' writing in and speaking about the genre (e.g., narrative, short story, poetry, drama, essay, website)

None of these approaches is inherently better than the others. Rather, we suggest that whichever approach you choose, you can begin with student learning needs to spiral instruction and therefore learning toward further complexity. For example, if you wanted to organize your units thematically, you might begin using answers to Figure 6.4 questions to identify a theme that you know your students will find engaging and relevant as they read and write texts around the theme throughout the unit. Reading Anchor Standard 9 deals specifically with thematic understanding, so you can ask students to wrestle with theme in each unit (in addition to targeting other standards) by building on the expectations from a previous unit. Through this process, students will have to apply prior learning to a new theme and texts with new, more complex skills, strategies, and thinking.

Choosing Resources

Connections

A useful and current definition of *text* clearly includes print materials such as novels, short stories, and poetry, but also expands to include other types of twenty-first-century documents such as newspaper and magazine articles, webpages, film and video, and even audio and sound clips. Expanding our notions of what counts as a text in classrooms is part of encouraging our students to develop multiple literacies. Sarah Brown Wessling's discussion of texts in Chapter 2 can help you think further about how we define and use fulcrum, textured, and context texts.

With an organizational scheme in mind, in the early stages of unit planning, teachers often consider the texts they will use in a unit. We recognize that many districts or schools have adopted core texts or fulcrum texts that serve as the foundation of particular units of study. Identifying these and other resources in support of a unit's focus that meets the CCSS demands is an important consideration. As our earlier discussions in Section I affirmed, it will be important to also consider when choosing resources that the CCSS do encourage the unification of ELA strand sets (reading, writing, speaking and listening, and language) so that each unit of study integrates standards from each strand set (see Figure 1.1).

We agree that teachers and students need greater access to a wider range of texts. Hopefully, the CCSS will raise awareness of why students would benefit from access to such materials, especially since the CCSS do raise awareness of the value of students' use of increasingly complex texts—both literature and informational. But we also acknowledge, based on our own experience, the range of choice that exists in different schools. For some of us, choice means selecting what is already available and finding free or reproducible alternatives when possible. For others, choice means the opportunity to order resources in support of unit objectives. There are unique challenges that each context poses. For those with little choice, considering how to help students meet the CCSS demands can seem nearly impossible.

Nonetheless, the discussion in Chapter 2 about the use of fulcrum, textured, and context texts highlights how you can use even a small sampling of various texts, even in different genres and modes to help students navigate complex texts. As we learn more about text complexity and the ways to help our students navigate these texts, we recognize that we will all need to at least begin with what we have in our resource shelves and rooms. But the issue of pressing import may be less about what materials we have than what we do or better yet what we ask students to do. We can best focus our energies on going more deeply with fewer texts of greater complexity than on breadth and coverage. Resource choices should be made in conjunction with choices about unit objectives and goals that will help students meet the CCSS and more.

Beginning with the End in Mind: Scaffolding Assessment throughout a Unit of Study

Because the CCSS are a set of grade-level expectations, they focus on outcomes. That is to say, the CCSS articulate what students should be able to do at the end of a particular grade. The CCSS as well as good unit design and planning suggest that we begin planning with the end in mind—that we keep omnipresent in our minds and on paper the ultimate goal we have for students. Figure 6.5, the Unit Plan Template, provides one frame for thinking through and logging your plans for a unit of study.

We suggest that once you've identified the focus for a particular unit of study, you begin by identifying the outcome of the unit or what students will be expected to do at the end of the unit. Your unit objectives and goals will help you articulate what learning or tasks students will be able to enact at the end of the unit. Put another way, you'll want to identify the summative assessment that you'll ask students

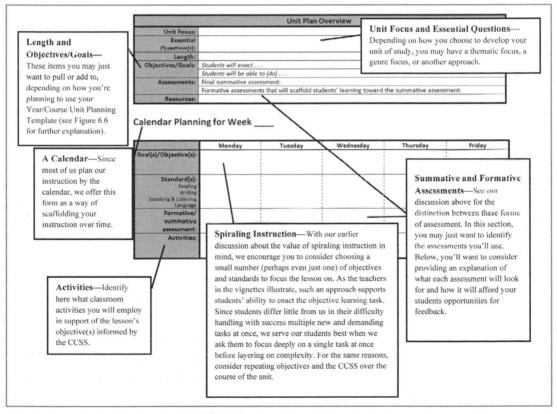

FIGURE 6.5: Unit plan template.

Web 6.1

to complete at the end of the unit. Summative assessments focus on reporting whether students have met proficiency in demonstrating their ability to enact unit objectives. Often, summative assessments take the form of essays or presentations, but as NCTE notes on www.ncte.org /books/supp-students-9-12, there are many other forms of summative assessments.

Although the CCSS are finally about what happens in the end, it is also important to note that the CCSS are not exhaustive. The CCSS need not limit the scope of your instruction. Yes, they set the minimum, but you can define the upper limits of your instruction and expectations for students as you plan instruction.

Similarly, it is critical to keep in mind that teacher-developed formative assessments will ultimately have the greatest influence on shaping the instruction and learning experiences that support students' ability to perform well on summative assessments. Multiple formative assessments strategically employed throughout a unit support ongoing learning and instruction. As the NCTE Research Policy Brief "Fostering High-Quality Formative Assessment" details, high-quality formative assessments offer students *and* teachers more immediate feedback on students' ability to enact a specific learning task. This feedback helps students know how and why they can proceed in working to enact the task or in progressing toward the next task (part of spiraling instruction and learning). For teachers, formative assessments inform instructional decision making and interventions in helping to ensure that all students are able to meet proficiency on the summative assessment task(s).

Given the instructional and learning value of formative assessments, you will want to identify the formative assessments you'll include in your unit of study. The formative assessments you identify and design should help both you and your students identify where, when, and how to intervene in support of their learning and ability to enact the objectives, or learning tasks, throughout the unit. The formative assessments you choose should therefore come at critical points in the unit where you will be asking students to try out or enact new and difficult tasks. As you may already know or infer from the discussion thus far, formative assessments are not focused on grading students. Rather, formative assessments are focused on providing you and your students with feedback that will guide subsequent teaching and learning. This feedback will influence, as you help them to see, their later successful performance on the summative assessment. Collectively, the formative assessments you scaffold throughout the unit should help build students' ability and confidence in demonstrating proficiency on the latter summative assessment(s).

Figure 6.5 and the pull-out boxes offer further details about the type of planning thoughts you might want to record as you build or revise a unit of study with the end in mind.

Planning and Organizing Units across the Year or Semester

Identifying individual units of study cannot occur without simultaneously considering how multiple units of study progress across the year or semester (depending on the grade level). As we have discussed, these considerations are a part of the spiraling that you can plan for across units of study. For example, teachers who choose a genre approach might begin with a personal narrative unit of study where students review prior learning from a previous course or grade level about reading thinking strategies and writing strategies for developing ideas. In a later short-story unit, teachers might spiral students' learning by revisiting reading and thinking strategies in this new genre to explore with students how readers approach different kinds of texts. At the same time, teachers could introduce greater complexity in one or more of the thinking strategies they ask students to enact. And in terms of writing instruction, teachers might spiral instruction by building on earlier ways they invited students to develop ideas within a paragraph to consider how idea development works across paragraphs complicated by learning how this works in a new genre.

As you develop individual units of study in relation to other units, Figure 6.6 can serve as a tool for logging how you plan to spiral instruction within and across units of study. The pull-out boxes below offer further details about the type of planning thoughts you might want to record in each box.

Just as instruction spirals across a unit of study, so too does formative assessment. As students encounter new and increasingly difficult tasks, immediate feedback via formative assessments helps to build students' confidence and commitment to the task at hand. This is because the formative assessment helps students identify which areas they need to focus on and teachers can clarify misunderstanding. Formative assessments therefore boost students' learning across a unit of study; these formative assessments support students' improvement over time and ability to negotiate increasingly demanding tasks with independence.

The chapters included in Section II provide a useful tool for thinking as you consider planning your own units of study. We do not offer them as packages to adopt; after all, such an approach might not take into consideration the unique contextual factors influencing your decision making, including most notably what you know about your students.

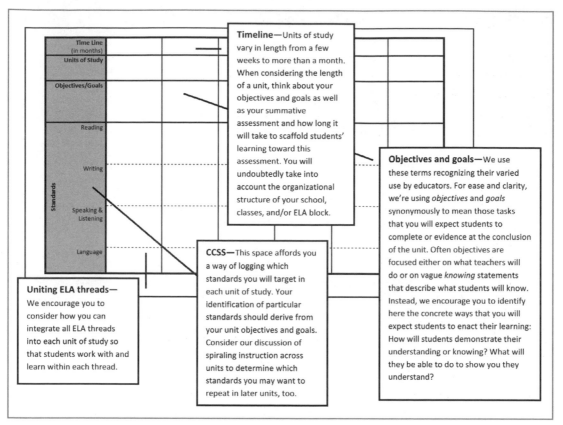

Time Line
(in months)

Units of Study

Objectives/Goals

Reading

Writing

Standards

Speaking &
Listening

Language

Timeline—Units of study vary in length from a few weeks to more than a month. When considering the length of a unit, think about your objectives and goals as well as your summative assessment and how long it will take to scaffold students' learning toward this assessment. You will undoubtedly take into account the organizational structure of your school, classes, and/or ELA block.

Objectives and goals—We use these terms recognizing their varied use by educators. For ease and clarity, we're using *objectives* and *goals* synonymously to mean those tasks that you will expect students to complete or evidence at the conclusion of the unit. Often objectives are focused either on what teachers will do or on vague *knowing* statements that describe what students will know. Instead, we encourage you to identify here the concrete ways that you will expect students to enact their learning: How will students demonstrate their understanding or knowing? What will they be able to do to show you they understand?

CCSS—This space affords you a way of logging which standards you will target in each unit of study. Your identification of particular standards should derive from your unit objectives and goals. Consider our discussion of spiraling instruction across units to determine which standards you may want to repeat in later units, too.

Uniting ELA threads—We encourage you to consider how you can integrate all ELA threads into each unit of study so that students work with and learn within each thread.

FIGURE 6.6: Year/course unit planning template.

Working Collaboratively to Enact the CCSS

7

A s we have mentioned throughout the book, planning and teaching are collaborative processes strengthened with the support of colleagues. In Chapter 6, we discussed how your ongoing journey with the CCSS will centrally involve the students in your classroom, but your ability to positively affect student learning is largely influenced by the relationships you foster with colleagues as well. In this chapter, we suggest ways that teachers can work collaboratively to support one another and thereby their students.

Collaborate on Literacy across the Curriculum

The teachers' voices represented in this book and our ongoing conversations with colleagues across the nation reveal just how imperative collaborative efforts to understand and enact the CCSS are to the sustainability of our joint efforts. Many teachers—and administrators— are surprised to learn that the CCSS themselves urge us toward such aims. As we discussed earlier in our overview of the CCSS document and in Section I, the CCSS argue on page 7 that students who are college and career ready ought to be able to respond to a range of disciplinary demands, tasks, audiences, and purposes for writing, reading, speaking, and listen-

Web 7.1
Go online for other resources for building schoolwide literacy initiatives.

ing. The CCSS inclusion of College and Career Readiness Anchor Standards at the 6–12 grade levels for literacy in history/social science, science, and technical subjects sends a strong message that *with* our colleagues in these other content areas we are jointly responsible for helping students navigate the range of these literacy demands. Therefore, the CCSS recognize what we ELA teachers have long understood: we alone cannot take on the burden of equipping students to become literate consumers and producers of *all* content area knowledge. When some teachers read on page 5 of the CCSS document that by twelfth grade, 30 percent of the sum of students' reading should be literary and the other 70 percent informational, they assume that this means that they will need to devote 70 percent of students' ELA course reading to informational texts. However, consistent with this literacy across the content areas focus, the CCSS footnote to the chart with these percentages indicates that these targets are representative of students' reading of diverse texts across courses throughout their school day. Similarly, the CCSS spell out that the sum of twelfth-grade students' writing should include students' writing in ELA *and* non-ELA settings so that 40 percent of students' writing across courses will be to persuade, 40 percent to explain, and 20 percent to convey experience. It is therefore important for us to work with colleagues across content areas to determine how best to jointly support students' reading and writing across the school day in the range of their coursework.

Look for Opportunities to Form Professional Learning Groups and Communities

Professional learning groups and communities are powerful locations for teacher growth, development, and collaboration. As you work collaboratively with your colleagues, grade-level band, and department, look for opportunities to initiate authentic, inquiry-driven professional learning communities. A professional learning group can be a place to house discussion about the CCSS, NCTE principles, NCTE policy briefs, or professional books. To help you begin imagining new ways to engage in collaboration at your school, we have provided a few possible suggestions. These various opportunities for collaboration can strengthen communities of learning as they address the CCSS.

Web 7.2

- *Start a Teachers as Readers book group.* Some professional learning communities are designed as book clubs. Members read and discuss children's and young adults' literature along with professional texts.

  - *Take advantage of collaborative spaces.* Departmental meetings can be great places to work collaboratively with colleagues. In some schools, this will mean rethinking current views about departmental meetings. Often, with the best intentions, these spaces focus primarily on logistical issues with little support for teachers to draw on their own backgrounds and styles and embrace the strengths and needs of their students, but department meetings can be spaces where professional planning is grounded in a commitment to the autonomy of knowledgeable teachers who make decisions for and with their students. With such a view, department meetings can be places where teachers engage in professional study and reflection that supports growth in the company of colleagues who are wrestling with similar issues.

- *Attend national conferences.* Attending professional conferences is a fabulous way for teachers to find space and support for focused reflection. Through these experiences, teachers share their great work and learn from others in ways that will ultimately enhance successful teaching in their home districts and schools. Conferences support teachers by giving them opportunities to become intellectually reinvigorated by engaging with colleagues from across the country.

- *Seek out online forums.* Online forums are another space for reflection and growth. Participating in such forums, teachers gain insights from across the country as they have opportunities to share their work and learn from others' classrooms. With other teachers, they address challenges, pose questions, provide insight, and find new ideas about practice, materials, and other resources.

Web 7.3

Plan, Develop, and Assess with the CCSS

The CCSS document details grade-specific expectations but questions about how students will be asked to demonstrate the standard-specific task of understanding are left to teachers' collective expertise. To be clear, the CCSS do not advocate for particular ELA pedagogy. Therefore, collaborating with colleagues in your school, district, region, and state can help you localize the CCSS; together you can interpret the CCSS language and plan to enact the CCSS grade-level expectations in the ways most responsive to your local context.

Connections

The Oak Park teachers in Section II demonstrate how teachers use their knowledge of their contexts and the needs of their students to develop their curricula, thereby "localizing the CCSS." As these teachers' practices illustrate, the CCSS need not overshadow the particularities of the places in which we all teach.

Identify Grade-Level Distinctions

Figure 7.1 builds on our conversations about how to read the CCSS document for grade-level differences. This model can help you and your colleagues extend your initial individual thinking about horizontal and vertical alignment in relation to the CCSS document. The figure serves as a tool for articulating how you will ask students to demonstrate grade-level distinctions and what they will look like in your classrooms. By noting in the boxes what language is added or changed in the progression from grade to grade and how this language might translate to instructional choices and student activities, Figure 7.1 can be used on three levels:

- Level 1: to identify CCSS Anchor Standards distinctions across grade levels
- Level 2: to identify the learning tasks that students will need to enact to demonstrate proficiency in meeting each standard

- Level 3: to identify what you'll ask your students to do to enact the CCSS articulated expectations; in this level, together you can identify common formative and summative assessments you might use within and/or across grade levels

You can therefore use this document three separate times or for three separate passes to examine and discuss each focus level. Or you could choose to focus on a single level that offers you a way to scaffold conversations with your colleagues. The textboxes below help to explain how Figure 7.1 can be used at each level.

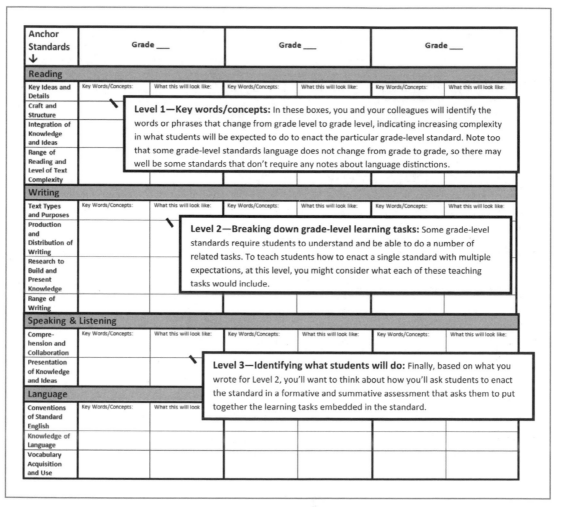

Anchor Standards ↓	Grade ___		Grade ___		Grade ___	
Reading						
Key Ideas and Details	Key Words/Concepts:	What this will look like:	Key Words/Concepts:	What this will look like:	Key Words/Concepts:	What this will look like:
Craft and Structure						
Integration of Knowledge and Ideas						
Range of Reading and Level of Text Complexity						
Writing						
Text Types and Purposes	Key Words/Concepts:	What this will look like:	Key Words/Concepts:	What this will look like:	Key Words/Concepts:	What this will look like:
Production and Distribution of Writing						
Research to Build and Present Knowledge						
Range of Writing						
Speaking & Listening						
Comprehension and Collaboration	Key Words/Concepts:	What this will look like:	Key Words/Concepts:	What this will look like:	Key Words/Concepts:	What this will look like:
Presentation of Knowledge and Ideas						
Language						
Conventions of Standard English	Key Words/Concepts:	What this will look				
Knowledge of Language						
Vocabulary Acquisition and Use						

Level 1—Key words/concepts: In these boxes, you and your colleagues will identify the words or phrases that change from grade level to grade level, indicating increasing complexity in what students will be expected to do to enact the particular grade-level standard. Note too that some grade-level standards language does not change from grade to grade, so there may well be some standards that don't require any notes about language distinctions.

Level 2—Breaking down grade-level learning tasks: Some grade-level standards require students to understand and be able to do a number of related tasks. To teach students how to enact a single standard with multiple expectations, at this level, you might consider what each of these teaching tasks would include.

Level 3—Identifying what students will do: Finally, based on what you wrote for Level 2, you'll want to think about how you'll ask students to enact the standard in a formative and summative assessment that asks them to put together the learning tasks embedded in the standard.

FIGURE 7.1: Grade-level distinctions planning template.

In Figure 7.2, we provide an example of how you might use this document at all three levels using Anchor Speaking and Listening Standard 4. The pull-outs highlight further the thinking at each level of discussion. It is important to note that this chart does not need to replace your existing tools and resources for mapping curriculum. Instead, it offers one way to help you think through the grade-level distinctions in conversations with others.

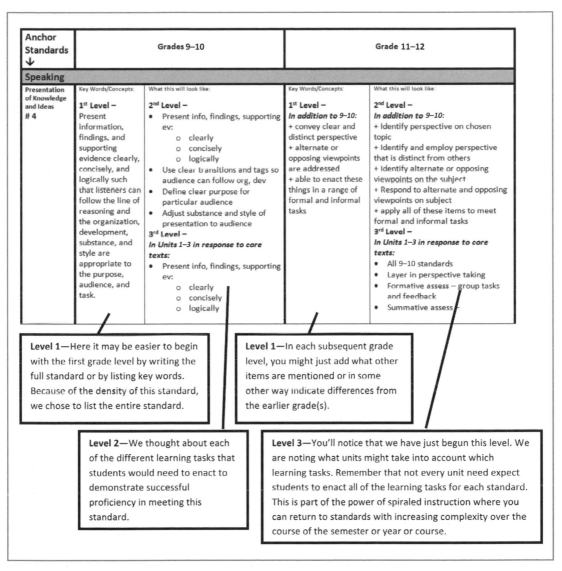

FIGURE 7.2: Grade-level distinctions example.

Plan Common Course or Grade-Level Instruction

Understanding the grade-level distinctions using Figure 7.1 might also encourage you to consider ways to plan instruction with others who teach the same course or grade level. You can focus together on integrating ELA threads as well. We encourage you to consider using Figures 6.5 and 6.6 to facilitate your discussions and plans with colleagues who teach the same grade level or course as well as department colleagues who can help you think about spiraling instruction from previous grades and courses for students.

Identify Common Texts

Meeting in grade level, course teams, or departments to develop units around core, or fulcrum, texts can be a useful way to align instruction with the CCSS. As the Oak Park teachers describe, using common texts can be a way to reorient your conversations toward students' ability to enact learning tasks and you can share common experiences to adapt instruction while still feeling at liberty to pick context and texture texts. Together you can ask questions as you begin planning about which texts to choose and why:

- What young adult novels, poems, nonfiction articles, or other texts could supplement fulcrum texts?
- How can we incorporate other ELA threads in our discussion of and writing about chosen texts?
- How can we integrate digital technology or multimodal opportunities for students to enact CCSS learning tasks as they read and compose texts?
- How can we support struggling or reluctant readers with the chosen fulcrum texts?

Select and Enact a New Teaching Strategy

As the Oak Park team also suggests, beyond planning together, trying out a new teaching strategy in your classroom can be easier when you do it with one or two other teachers. The CCSS invite teachers to study how particular instructional practices support student learning and ability to demonstrate proficiency in meeting and exceeding the CCSS expectations. If your building has a literacy specialist or lead literacy teacher, you can ask him or her to help you plan and give you feedback or you can build a study group focused on action research with other colleagues. Once you try out the new strategy, evaluate the results using joint learning goals and objectives, and work together to tweak and repeat. Your group can also share your results with your grade-level group or department.

Develop Common Assessments

Level 3 of Figure 7.1, as the example in Figure 7.2 begins, invites you to consider how you might collaboratively identify, develop, and adapt common formative and summative assessments within grade levels or courses taught by more than one teacher. As the Oak Park teachers describe, they use common assessments to review their instruction as well as students' work throughout units of study. Because they share the assessments and the language, making adjustments to instruction in the midst of units and in relation to future units becomes a shared responsibility. In this way, these teachers remain ever responsive to their students' learning needs and ultimately to their students' ability to enact unit learning tasks that demonstrate their ability to meet the CCSS demands.

Share Ideas Online with Colleagues Near and Far

We encourage you to share your efforts and ideas in online professional forums and with your colleagues in your professional learning communities. Because all of the figures and charts throughout this book are also available for your use and adaptation on www.ncte.org/books/supp-students-9-12, we hope you will share your thinking related to, experiences using, and revision of these resources and your thoughts about the CCSS more generally there. Supporting one another online in such a forum is one way to strengthen our ability to help students meet the CCSS demands and to remind ourselves that colleagues nationwide are negotiating similar challenges. You can also find interactive lesson plans at www.readwritethink.org, or contribute some of your own.

Web 7.4

In a profession where we all largely perform the obligations and duties of our role as ELA teachers alone in our classrooms, it is critically important to remember that you are not alone in this effort to enact the CCSS. We hope the teachers you've met in Section II highlight the powerful potential of uniting with others who share the challenge of meeting the CCSS demands.

8

Becoming a Teacher Advocate

The teachers featured in Section II highlight powerful ways of leveraging the CCSS to shape instruction that meets students' needs and prepares them to contribute to a world we can only imagine today. These teachers, however, are but a few of the thousands of committed ELA K–12 teachers who share this goal, including you. Part of your strength and expertise as an ELA teacher and/or instructional leader is your ability to advocate for your own professional needs and therefore your students' learning needs in collaboration with others near and far. Your commitment to reading this book, to learning about how the CCSS intersect with your teaching practices, and to working with others to learn and plan together illustrates your concern for keeping students at the center.

Throughout this book we have discussed ways in which you can work individually and collaboratively to make sense of, put into perspective, and act in relation to the CCSS; in this brief final section we invite you to begin considering how you can work to advocate locally, within your state, and even nationally in equally important small and large ways for the support that will enable you to sustain the professional learning and practices in support of students' needs. Below we highlight by building on earlier conversations ways that you can begin this advocacy work.

Advocate for Yourself by Committing to Continued Professional Growth

Every teacher knows that professional autonomy is not a given. When discussing standards or other guidelines, it is important to be alert to tendencies to look at the CCSS as a means to homogenize ways of teaching and students' pathways to learning. At the same time, teachers have a responsibility to meet their side of the bargain. As teachers, we cannot claim the right to autonomy without committing to ongoing, focused professional growth.

Advocate for Your Students by Using Knowledge of Your Context to Design Instruction

Rigid interpretations of standards often lead to the imposition of rigid pacing guides and scripted programs that tell teachers what to do and say. Scripted programs limit what teachers can do in their classrooms by failing to draw on their professional knowledge. Work together in schools and districts to ensure that standards are used knowledgeably and responsibly so that policies never deny teachers their ability to use their professional knowledge.

Advocate for Instruction That Is Student Centered

We know that using the cultural heritages, orientations, and resources of ethnically and racially diverse students helps them learn. Seek, find, celebrate, and utilize the rich languages and literacies that exist in the homes and communities of your students. Students also bring diverse learning styles and enormous variations and abilities; consider these in developing instruction. Fill your classroom and the halls of your schools with wide varieties of languages, literacies, and abilities. Teach about them and teach through them. Because our choice in resources ought to be guided by the overarching goals and purposes that guide our planning units of study, we can best persuade internal and external stakeholders about the worth and necessity of such resources when we can also provide a compelling rationale. The best rationale centers on student achievement.

Advocate for the Use of Locally Developed Formative Assessments

It is critically important to recognize your professional expertise in developing formative assessments that speak with specificity to your students' learning needs. You know the local needs of your students and the community that supports their learning in and out of school. Therefore, you and your colleagues are best suited to design, implement, and adjust the formative assessments that will best enable your students to meet the demands of the CCSS. Speaking with colleagues both near and far will enable you to speak compellingly with local and national stakeholders about how your locally designed, implemented, and adjusted formative assessments best meet your students' needs and are still responsive to the CCSS.

Advocate for Your Students by Contributing to Larger Professional Communities

When our days are consumed by the immediate needs of our students and colleagues, it can feel overwhelming to think of joining other colleagues from afar. Alternately, you may wonder what you have to contribute to a larger professional community beyond your school or district. But you can rest assured that the time and energy necessary to do so are well worth it and less extensive than you might think. You do have a lot to share with others; your experiences are worthy of others' attention. And professional organizations such as NCTE are a renewing space to remind yourself of this and to find solace and empowerment, especially as you meet the challenges of the CCSS.

We share your concern about the onslaught of attacks against teachers, including ELA teachers, by those who question our professional knowledge. Connecting with others near and far to give voice to your expertise is one amazingly powerful way to begin speaking back persuasively. And in this time of the CCSS, we believe in the work illustrated by the teachers featured in Section II and similarly enacted by teachers like you across this country. Your teaching practices and efforts to keep students at the center illustrate that the CCSS can be leveraged toward powerful ends by those of us who do the work that matters daily with the students in our lives. By connecting with one another locally, regionally, and nationally, we have the power to influence what the CCSS will become by joining the conversation. But it's more than just connecting. By equipping ourselves with the knowledge that comes from observing the CCSS deeply and from centering our CCSS-informed instruction on our knowledge of local contexts, we can join with teachers locally, nationally, and internationally in building instructional practices that will enable students to develop the habits that lead to becoming flexible, adaptive readers, writers, thinkers, and doers who are ready to meet the challenges of the twenty-first century.

Appendix A

Resources

Following is a consolidation of professional resources provided throughout and in support of the issues and concepts discussed in this text. These resources could serve educators' ongoing discussions, study groups, and individual inquiries equally well.

Topic	Resource
Critical and visual literacies	Freebody, P. (1992). A socio-cultural approach: Resourcing four roles as a literacy learner. In A. Watson & A. Badenhop (Eds.), *Prevention of reading failure* (pp. 48–60). Sydney: Ashton-Scholastic. Freebody, P., & Luke, A. (1990). Literacies programs: Debates and demands in cultural context. *Prospect: Australian Journal of TESOL, 5*(7), 7–16.
	Golden, J. (2001). *Reading in the dark: Using film as a tool in the English classroom*. Urbana: NCTE. Golden, J. (2006). *Reading in the reel world: Teaching documentaries and other nonfiction texts*. Urbana: NCTE.
	Pahl, K., & Roswell, J. (2005). *Literacy and education: Understanding the new literacy studies in the classroom*. Thousand Oaks, CA: Sage.
	Patel Stevens, L., & Bean, T. W. (2007). *Critical literacy: Context, research, and practice in the K–12 classroom*. Thousand Oaks, CA: Sage.
Developing and supporting professional learning communities	Cochran-Smith, M., & Lytle, S. L. (2009). *Inquiry as stance: practitioner research for the next generation*. New York: Teachers College Press.
	Lent, R. C. (2007). *Literacy learning communities: A guide for creating sustainable change in secondary schools*. Portsmouth: Heinemann.
	NCTE. *Pathways professional development*. Retrieved from http://www.ncte.org/pathways

Topic	Resource
Digital literacies and Web 2.0 instruction	Kajder, S. (2010). *Adolescents and digital literacies: Learning alongside our students*. Urbana: NCTE.
	National Writing Project, DeVoss, D. N., Eidman-Aadahl, E., & Hicks, T. (2010). *Because digital writing matters*. San Francisco: Jossey-Bass.
English language arts instruction	Bomer, R. (2011). *Building adolescent literacy in today's English classrooms*. Portsmouth: Heinemann.
	International Reading Association & NCTE. *ReadWriteThink*. Retrieved from http://www.readwritethink.org/
	Wilhelm, J. D., & Novak, B. (2011). *Teaching literacy for love and wisdom: Being the book and being the change*. New York: Teachers College Press, NCTE, and NWP.
Instructional approaches	Appleman, D. (2008). *Critical encounters in high school English: Teaching literacy theory to adolescents*. New York: Teachers College Press & NCTE.
	Fisher, N., & Frey, D. *Literacy for life*. Retrieved from http://www.fisherandfrey.com/
	Kleon, A. (2010). *Newspaper blackout*. New York: Harper.
Literacy coaching	Toll, C. (2006). *The literacy coach's desk reference: Process and perspectives for effective coaching*. Urbana: NCTE.
Literacy across content areas and school-wide literacy initiatives	Beers, K., Probst, R., & Rief, L. (Eds.). (2007). *Adolescent literacy: Turning promise into practice*. Portsmouth: Heinemann.
	Gere, A. R., Dickinson, H., Orzulak, M. M., & Moody, S. (2010). *Taking initiative on writing: A guide for instructional leaders*. Urbana: NCTE.
	Rush, L., Eakle, A. J., & Berger, A. (Eds.). (2007). *Secondary school literacy: What research reveals for classroom practice*. Urbana: NCTE.
Reading instruction and secondary readers	Appleman, D. (2010). *Adolescent literacy and the teaching of reading: Lessons for teachers of literature*. Urbana: NCTE.
	Campbell, K. H. (2007). *Less is more: Teaching literature with short texts—grades 6–12*. Portland: Stenhouse.
	Smith, M. W., & Wilhelm, J. D. (2009). *Fresh takes on teaching literary elements: How to teach what really matters about character, setting, point of view, and theme*. Urbana: NCTE & Scholastic.

Topic	Resource
Special student populations	Fisher, D., Rothenberg, C., & Frey, N. (2007). *Language learners in the English classroom*. Urbana: NCTE.
	Redd, T., & Webb, K. S. (2005). *A teacher's introduction to African American English: What a writing teacher should know*. Urbana: NCTE.
Standards and policy issues	NCTE James R. Squire Office of Policy Research. Policy briefs. Retrieved from http://www.ncte.org/policy-research Specifically the "Fostering High-Quality Formative Assessment," https://secure.ncte.org/store/formative-assessment
	Newmann, F. M., King, M. B., & Carmichael, D. L. (2007). *Authentic instruction and assessment: Common standards for rigor and relevance in teaching academic subjects*. Des Moines: State of Iowa Department of Education.
	Sipe, R. (2009). *Adolescent literacy at risk? The impact of standards*. Urbana: NCTE.
Writing instruction and secondary writers	Dean, D. (2008). *Genre theory: Teaching, writing, and being*. Urbana: NCTE.
	Fecho, B. (2011). *Writing in the dialogical classroom: Students and teachers responding to the texts of their lives*. Urbana: NCTE.
	Hillocks, G. J. (2011). *Teaching argument writing, grades 6–12: Supporting claims with relevant evidence and clear reasoning*. Portsmouth: Heinemann.

Appendix B

NCTE Principles

Throughout this book, there have been references to the NCTE Principles that guide inspiring and effective teachers such as those featured in the vignettes. Drawn from research and based on classroom practices that foster student learning, these Principles provide the foundation on which excellent teaching and enhanced student learning is built. This section includes explanations of NCTE Principles about several areas of instruction—reading, writing, speaking and listening, and language—along with principles on formative assessment, teaching English language learners, 21st century literacies, and the role of teachers as decision-makers in planning and implementing instruction. This last is the overarching principle under which all the others are clustered because it speaks to the heart of teacher work.

The Principles in this appendix represent a compilation of work created and endorsed by NCTE, much of which can be found and is referenced on the NCTE website. As you think about ways to begin planning and shifting your instruction to align with the CCSS, use this document as a reference and resource, grounding your instruction, as well, in established, research-based NCTE principles. Each set of principles is organized into two categories: what NCTE knows about learners and learning, and what that knowledge means for teachers in the classroom.

NCTE Principles Regarding Teachers as Decision-Makers

A number of NCTE documents affirm the role of teachers as decision-makers. Among the most recent are the 2005 "Features of Literacy Programs: A Decision-Making Matrix," produced by the Commission on Reading; the 2008 Resolution passed by the Board of Directors on Scripted Curricula; and the 2010 Resolution on Affirming the Role of Teachers and Students in Developing Curriculum.

Both the CCSS and NCTE agree that teachers' professional judgment and experience should shape the way that the goals inherent in the CCSS will be reached. Common agreement on what students should be able to accomplish leaves ample room for teachers to make decisions about the materials and strategies that will be used in the classroom. Teachers are not simply implementation agents for the CCSS; rather, they are active shapers of schoolwide plans that will enable students to reach the goals of these or any standards.

The journeys recounted in this book demonstrate that teachers work, learn, and plan most effectively when they collaborate with their colleagues. Indeed, research shows that teaching teams are a vital unit of school change and improvement.

What we know about teaching as a profession:

Working in teams allows teachers to design and share goals and strategies, strengthens the foundation for informed decision making, and contributes to participation in more broadly based communities of practice. Teaching teams bring together teachers, administrators, and other educators to:

- Develop and assess curricula
- Assess and become more knowledgeable about student learning
- Design and support activities that enhance professional practice
- Apply cross-disciplinary perspectives to curriculum design, assessment, and professional growth
- Conduct collective inquiry into the learning and teaching environment
- Connect to parents and the community

We also know that teaching is a professional endeavor, and that teachers are active problem-solvers and decision-makers in the classroom. As professionals, teachers and students benefit from sustained and empowering professional development for teachers.

What this means for educators:

- Administrators and teacher leaders should provide for systematic professional development as an essential component of successful school reform. Teachers who have opportunities for quality professional development are best able to help students learn.

- We need to collectively define teacher effectiveness as professional practice that uses deep content knowledge, effective pedagogy, authentic formative assessments, connections with parents and communities, sustained reflection, and research-based practices to engage students and help them learn.

- Schools should support a comprehensive literacy policy as described in the Literacy Education for All, Results for the Nation (LEARN) Act that requires a sustained investment in literacy learning and instruction from birth through grade 12 and empowers teachers to design and select formative assessments and lessons.

NCTE Principles Regarding Reading Instruction

The original version of this NCTE Guideline, titled "On Reading, Learning to Read, and Effective Reading Instruction: An Overview of What We Know and How We Know It," can be found on NCTE's website at http://www.ncte.org/positions/statements/onreading and was authored by The Commission on Reading of the National Council of Teachers of English.

As the teachers in this volume have demonstrated, reading instruction consumes a lot of our attention in the classroom. The creators of the CCSS have acknowledged the importance of literacy for twenty-first-century learners by including standards for literacy instruction across content areas; indeed, as reading materials become more diverse and complex in this digital age, we need to prepare our students to encounter different types of texts in different situations.

What we know about reading and learning to read:

- Reading is a complex and purposeful sociocultural, cognitive, and linguistic process in which readers simultaneously use their knowledge of spoken and written language, their knowledge of the topic of the text, and their knowledge of their culture to construct meaning with text.
- Readers read for different purposes.
- As children learn to read continuous text, they use their intuitive knowledge of spoken language and their knowledge of the topic to figure out print words in text.
- The more children read, the better readers they become.
- Children read more when they have access to engaging, age-appropriate books, magazines, newspapers, computers, and other reading materials. They read more on topics that interest them than on topics that do not interest them.
- Reading supports writing development and writing supports reading development.
- All readers use their life experiences, their knowledge of the topic, and their knowledge of oral and written language to make sense of print.
- Readers continue to grow in their ability to make sense of an increasing variety of texts on an increasing variety of topics throughout their lives.

What this means for teachers of reading:

- Teachers should know their students as individuals, including their interests, their attitudes about reading, and their school, home, and community experiences.

- Teachers should read to students daily using a variety of text types.
- Teachers should try to use a variety of instructional groupings, including whole-group, small-group, and individual instruction, to provide multiple learning experiences.
- Teachers should teach before-, during-, and after-reading strategies for constructing meaning of written language, including demonstrations and think-alouds.
- Teachers should provide specific feedback to students to support their reading development.
- Teachers should provide regular opportunities for students to respond to reading through discussion, writing, art, drama, storytelling, music, and other creative expressions.
- Teachers should provide regular opportunities for students to reflect on their learning.
- Teachers should gradually release instructional responsibility to support independent reading.
- Teachers need to reflect on their students' progress and their own teaching practices to make changes that meet the needs of students.

NCTE Principles Regarding
the Teaching of Writing

The original version of this NCTE Guideline, titled "NCTE Beliefs about the Teaching of Writing," can be found on NCTE's website at http://www.ncte.org/positions/statements/writingbeliefs. It was originally authored by the Writing Study Group of the NCTE Executive Committee.

Just as the nature of and expectation for literacy has changed in the past century and a half, so has the nature of writing. Much of that change has been due to technological developments, from pen and paper, to typewriter, to word processor, to networked computer, to design software capable of composing words, images, and sounds. These developments not only expanded the types of texts that writers produce, but they also expanded immediate access to a wider variety of readers. The CCSS acknowledge this reality with standards that note the need for students to be able to use technology critically and effectively in their writing, but it is up to teachers to decide how to engage students with meaningful writing tasks that will enable them to meet the demands of our quickly changing society.

What we know about writing and learning to write:

- Everyone has the capacity to write, writing can be taught, and teachers can help students become better writers.
- People learn to write by writing.
- Writing is a process and a tool for thinking.
- Writing grows out of many different purposes.
- Conventions of finished and edited texts are important to readers and therefore to writers.
- Writing and reading are related.
- Literate practices are embedded in complicated social relationships.
- Composing occurs in different modalities and technologies.
- Assessment of writing involves complex, informed, human judgment.

What this means for teachers of writing:

- Writing instruction must include ample in-class and out-of-class opportunities for writing and should include writing for a variety of purposes and audiences.

- Instruction should be geared toward making sense in a life outside of school.

- Writing instruction must provide opportunities for students to identify the processes that work best for themselves as they move from one writing situation to another.

- Writing instruction must take into account that a good deal of workplace writing and other writing takes place in collaborative situations.

- It is important that teachers create opportunities for students to be in different kinds of writing situations, where the relationships and agendas are varied.

- Simply completing workbook or online exercises is inadequate.

- Students should have access to and experience in reading material that presents both published and student writing in various genres.

- Students should be taught the features of different genres experientially, not only explicitly.

- The teaching of writing should assume students will begin with the sort of language with which they are most at home and most fluent in their speech.

- Writing instruction must accommodate the explosion in technology from the world around us.

- Instructors must recognize the difference between formative and summative evaluation and be prepared to evaluate students' writing from both perspectives.

NCTE Principles Regarding
Speaking and Listening

NCTE principles on speaking and listening are articulated in "Guideline on the Essentials of English," which can be found at http://www.ncte.org/positions/statements/essentialsofenglish.

NCTE has a long history of supporting both instruction and assessment that integrates speaking and listening skills into the teaching of the English language arts, and the CCSS acknowledge the importance of speaking and listening in their Speaking and Listening Standards. Speaking refers to both informal speech such as talking in small groups or participating in class discussions and formal speech that results from composing and presenting a text. Listening means engaging in a complex active process that serves a variety of purposes.

What we know about speaking and listening in school:

- Public speaking is consistently ranked as one of the greatest sources of anxiety for people of all ages, and students are no exception.
- Much of the work of the classroom is done through speaking and listening.
- Formal speaking can be extemporaneous, relying on detailed notes but no actual script, or text-based.
- If students spend discussion time competing for the attention of the teacher rather than listening and responding to peers, they will not benefit from the informal speech in the classroom.
- It can be difficult to evaluate listening.
- One of the advantages of speaking is that it can generate immediate response, and it is important to make full use of this feature.

What this means for teachers of speaking and listening:

- To ensure that all students have an opportunity to develop skills of informal speech, teachers should not depend exclusively on volunteers in class discussion.
- Strategies for broadening participation include having all students respond in writing and then asking each student to respond aloud, asking students to discuss in pairs and report to the class, or distributing "talk tokens" that students can turn in after a contribution to a class discussion.

- Teachers should support the development of formal speaking and provide students with support and opportunities to practice so that they can feel well-prepared.
- Teachers need to give explicit attention to the connections between speaking and listening.
- To foster active listening, teachers can encourage students to build upon one another's contributions to discussions or require them to write a brief summary of the discussion at the end of class.

NCTE Principles Regarding Language Instruction

. . . .

A comprehensive statement of NCTE's principles on language instruction appears in "Learning through Language: A Call for Action in All Disciplines," which can be found on NCTE's website at http://www.ncte.org/positions/statements/ learningthroughlang. It was prepared by NCTE's Language and Learning across the Curriculum Committee.

Language is a primary way individuals communicate what they think and feel. They find self-identity through language, shape their knowledge and experiences by means of it, and depend on it as a lifelong resource for expressing their hopes and feelings. One of the goals of language instruction is to foster language awareness among students so that they will understand how language varies in a range of social and cultural settings; how people's attitudes toward language vary across culture, class, gender, and generation; how oral and written language affects listeners and readers; how conventions in language use reflect social-political-economic values; how the structure of language works; and how first and second languages are acquired. The CCSS provide standards for language instruction, but teachers should use their knowledge of language to help foster an interest in language that is contextually bound to other literate practices.

What we know about language and learning language:

- As human beings, we can put sentences together even as children—we can all do grammar.

- Students make errors in the process of learning, and as they learn about writing, they often make new errors, not necessarily fewer ones.

- Students benefit much more from learning a few grammar keys thoroughly than from trying to remember many terms and rules.

- Students find grammar most interesting when they apply it to authentic texts.

- Inexperienced writers find it difficult to make changes in the sentences that they have written.

- All native speakers of a language have more grammar in their heads than any grammar book will ever contain.

What this means for teachers of language:

- Teachers should foster an understanding of grammar and usage.
- Instructors must integrate language study into all areas of the English language arts.
- Teachers should experiment with different approaches to language instruction until they find the ones that work the best for them and their students.
- Teachers should show students how to apply grammar not only to their writing but also to their reading and to their other language arts activities.
- Teachers can make good use of the other languages and the various dialects of English in their classrooms.
- Teachers might try using texts of different kinds, such as newspapers and the students' own writing, as sources for grammar examples and exercises.
- Teachers should use grammar exercises that improve writing, such as sentence combining and model sentences.

NCTE Principles Regarding Teaching English Language Learners

The original version of this NCTE Guideline, entitled "NCTE Position Paper on the Role of English Teachers in Educating English Language Learners (ELLs)," can be found on NCTE's website at http://www.ncte.org/positions /statements/teacherseducatingell. It was originally authored by members of the ELL Task Force: Maria Brisk, Stephen Cary, Ana Christina DaSilva Iddings, Yu Ren Dong, Kathy Escamilla, Maria Franquiz, David Freeman, Yvonne Freeman, Paul Kei Matsuda, Christina Ortmeier-Hooper, David Schwarzer, Katie Van Sluys, Randy Bomer (EC Liaison), and Shari Bradley (Staff Liaison).

Multilingual students differ in various ways, including level of oral English proficiency, literacy ability in both the heritage language and English, and cultural background. English language learners born in the United States often develop conversational language abilities in English but lack academic language proficiency. Newcomers, on the other hand, need to develop both conversational and academic English. The creators of the CCSS note that the standards do not address the needs of English language learners (p. 6), but they also note that it is important for schools to consider and accommodate these students' needs while meeting the standards. These principles can provide a guide for teachers as they imagine what this might look like in their classrooms.

What we know about teaching multilingual learners:

- The academic language that students need in the different content areas differs.

- English language learners need three types of knowledge to become literate in a second language: the second language, literacy, and world knowledge.

- Second language acquisition is a gradual developmental process and is built on students' knowledge and skill in their native language.

- Bilingual students also need to learn to read and write effectively to succeed in school.

- Writing well in English is often the most difficult skill for English language learners to master.

- English language learners may not be familiar with terminology and routines often associated with writing instruction in the United States, including writing process, drafting, revision, editing, workshop, conference, audience, purpose, or genre.

What this means for teachers of multilingual students:

- For English language learners, teachers need to consider content objectives as well as English language development objectives.
- Because teachers relate to students both as learners and as children or adolescents, teachers must establish how they will address these two types of relationships, what they need to know about their students, and how they will acquire this knowledge.
- Teachers should provide authentic opportunities to use language in a nonthreatening environment.
- Teachers should encourage academic oral language in the various content areas.
- Teachers should give attention to the specific features of language students need to communicate in social as well as academic contexts.
- Teachers should include classroom reading materials that are culturally relevant.
- Teachers should ask families to read with students a version in the heritage language.
- Teachers should teach language features, such as text structure, vocabulary, and text- and sentence-level grammar, to facilitate comprehension of the text
- Teachers should give students frequent meaningful opportunities for them to generate their own texts.
- Teachers should provide models of well-organized papers for the class.

NCTE Principles Regarding 21st Century Literacies

The original version of this Position Statement, titled "21st Century Curriculum and Assessment Framework," can be found on NCTE's website at http://www.ncte.org/positions/statements/21stcentframework. It was adopted by the NCTE executive committee on November 19, 2008.

Literacy has always been a collection of cultural and communicative practices shared among members of particular groups. These literacies—from reading online newspapers to participating in virtual classrooms—are multiple, dynamic, and malleable. Students need to be able to navigate the multiple literacy situations in which they will find themselves, and undoubtedly, they already engage with a number of literacies that were not available to their parents and teachers. The CCSS include standards for students' effective and critical use of technology, and the following principles can help teachers consider how to implement instruction that will empower students as technology continues to change and affect their literacies.

What we know about 21st century literacies and learning:

- As society and technology change, so does literacy.
- Because technology has increased the intensity and complexity of literate environments, the twenty-first century demands that a literate person possess a wide range of abilities and competencies, many literacies.
- Students in the twenty-first century need interpersonal skills to work collaboratively in both face-to-face and virtual environments to use and develop problem-solving skills.
- Students in the twenty-first century must be aware of the global nature of our world and be able to select, organize, and design information to be shared, understood, and distributed beyond their classrooms.
- Students in the twenty-first century must be able to take information from multiple places and in a variety of different formats, determine its reliability, and create new knowledge from that information.
- Students in the twenty-first century must be critical consumers and creators of multimedia texts.
- Students in the twenty-first century must understand and adhere to legal and ethical practices as they use resources and create information.

What this means for teachers of twenty-first-century learners:

- Students should use technology as a tool for communication, research, and creation of new works.
- Students should find relevant and reliable sources that meet their needs.
- Teachers should encourage students to take risks and try new things with tools available to them.
- Teachers should create situations and assignments in which students work in a group in ways that allow them to create new knowledge or to solve problems that can't be created or solved individually.
- Students should work in groups of members with diverse perspectives and areas of expertise.
- Students should be given opportunities to share and publish their work in a variety of ways.
- Teachers should help students analyze the credibility of information and its appropriateness in meeting their needs.
- Students should have the tools to critically evaluate their own and others' multimedia works.

NCTE Principles Regarding Assessment

The original version of this document, titled "Standards for the Assessment of Reading and Writing, Revised Edition (2009)," can be found on NCTE's website at http://www.ncte.org/standards/assessmentstandards. This document was authored by members of the Joint IRA–NCTE Task Force on Assessment, Peter Johnston (chair), Peter Afflerbach, Sandra Krist, Kathryn Mitchell Pierce, Elizabeth Spalding, Alfred W. Tatum, and Sheila W. Valencia.

Assessment is an integral part of instruction, and NCTE affirms its importance for student learning. In particular, formative assessment can be a powerful means of improving student achievement because it is assessment *for* learning, but it must adhere to key principles to be effective. These principles include emphasizing timely and task-focused feedback because it is feedback, not the absence of a grade, that characterizes effective formative assessment; shaping instructional decisions based on student performance in formative assessment; embedding formative assessment in instruction because the use of a given instrument of assessment, not the instrument itself, confers value on formative assessment; and offering students increased opportunities to understand their own learning. The principles below, developed in collaboration with the International Reading Association, suggest how assessment, both formative and summative, can enhance student achievement.

What we know about assessment:

- Assessment experiences at all levels, whether formative or summative, have consequences for students.
- Assessment should emphasize what students can do rather than what they cannot do.
- Assessment must provide useful information to inform and enable reflection.
- If any individual student's interests are not served by an assessment practice, regardless of whether it is intended for administration or decision making by an individual or by a group, then that practice is not valid for that student.
- The most productive and powerful assessments for students are likely to be the formative assessments that occur in the daily activities of the classroom.
- The teacher is the most important agent of assessment.
- Teachers need to feel safe to share, discuss, and critique their own work with others.
- Teacher knowledge cannot be replaced by standardized tests.
- The primary purpose of assessment is to improve teaching and learning.

What this means for teachers:

- Teachers should be able to demonstrate how their assessment practices benefit and do not harm individual students.

- Teachers must be aware of and deliberate about their roles as assessors.

- Teachers must have routines for systematic assessment to ensure that each student is benefiting optimally from instruction.

- Teacher leaders and administrators need to recognize that improving teachers' assessment expertise requires ongoing professional development, coaching, and access to professional learning communities. Nurturing such communities must be a priority for improving assessment.

- Teachers must take responsibility for making and sharing judgments about students' achievements and progress.

- Teachers should give students multiple opportunities to talk about their writing.

- Schools and teachers must develop a trusting relationship with the surrounding community.

Sarah Brown Wessling

As a twelve-year veteran of the high school English language arts classroom, **Sarah Brown Wessling** has enjoyed working with all kinds of students throughout a spectrum of courses. She earned bachelor's and master's degrees from Iowa State University in English education and English literature, respectively. She also became a National Board Certified Teacher in 2005. Active in her district and state in professional development efforts, Wessling has served on numerous committees, special teams, and advisory boards. She has been especially active with the Iowa and National Council of Teachers of English, and has served as ICTE president. In 2010 Wessling was selected as the National Teacher of the Year and spent the year traveling nationally and internationally as a spokesperson for education. Having had hundreds of engagements around the country during that time, she says that the experience has "made [her] feel more responsible than ever to be a better teacher tomorrow." She returned to Johnston High School in 2011. Sarah and her husband, Tim, relish their favorite role as parents to Evan, Lauren, and Zachary at home in Johnston, Iowa.

Contributing Authors

Danielle Lillge's teaching experiences in England and Wisconsin have afforded her opportunities to learn from diverse students and colleagues. Drawing on her days as a student in Germany, New York, Michigan, and Wisconsin, Lillge continues, through her teaching, to challenge her thinking about educational equity issues. She earned a bachelor's degree and teaching certificate in English from St. Norbert College, De Pere, Wisconsin, and a master's degree in English education from the University of Michigan, Ann Arbor. After initiating a schoolwide literacy effort with colleagues at her high school, she served as a literacy coach. She also works with teachers in other school districts as a literacy specialist. Currently, Lillge is a doctoral student in the Joint PhD Program in English and Education at the University of Michigan, where she is pursuing questions about secondary writing across content areas that originated in her collaborations with high school colleagues.

Crystal VanKooten is an instructor of English composition and a graduate student in the Joint PhD Program in English and Education at the University of Michigan. She earned a bachelor's degree in English and Spanish secondary education from Calvin College, Grand Rapids, Michigan, and a master's degree in literature and culture from Oregon State University. She then taught high school English and Spanish at Century High School in Hillsboro, Oregon, for five years, where students first introduced her to the idea of exploring the intersections between reading, writing, and technologies through blogging about literature. VanKooten's current areas of research include theories of new media writing, digital literacies, and multimodal composition, and she loves finding ways to challenge students to compose purposefully through language and through multiple modes of expression in the writing classroom.

This book was typeset in TheMix and Palatino by Precision Graphics.

The typeface used on the cover is Myriad Pro.

The book was printed on 60-lb. White Recycled Opaque Offset paper by Versa Press, Inc.

30% Total Recycled Fiber